PASTORAL PERSPECTIVES

PASTORAL PERSPECTIVES

Insights for Shepherds of God's Flock

Les Lofquist

SHEPHERDS PRESS

Cary, North Carolina

Pastoral Perspectives: Insights for Shepherds of God's Flock

Copyright © 2025 by Les Lofquist

All rights reserved. No part of this publication may be reproduced, stored in a retrieval system, or transmitted in any form or by any means—electronic, mechanical, photocopy, recording, or any other—except for brief quotations in printed reviews, without the prior permission of the publisher.

Editorial assistance by Marcia Love
Interior design and layout by Marcus Corder
Cover photo by Pawan Sharma; design by Marcus Corder

Published by Shepherds Press
6051 Tryon Road
Cary, NC 27518

Printed in the United States of America on acid-free paper.

ISBN: 978-1-959454-06-9 (paperback)

Unless otherwise indicated, all Scripture quotations are from The ESV® Bible (The Holy Bible, English Standard Version®), © 2001 by Crossway, a publishing ministry of Good News Publishers. Used by permission. All rights reserved.

Twenty-one chapters of this book were originally published in *VOICE*, the official publication of IFCA International. These chapters are 3, 4, 5, 7, 8, 9, 10, 11, 13, 14, 15, 16, 17, 18, 19, 20, 21, 23, 25, 26, and 27. Used by permission. All rights reserved.

For the glory of God
through the encouragement and support of my beloved wife, Miriam,
and our five children Anna, Chris, Paul, Amy, and Emily.

CONTENTS

Preface ix

Section 1: Perspectives on Pastoral Leadership

1. A Biblical Theology of Leadership 3
2. Components for a Philosophy of Leadership 10
3. Serious Ministry in a World of Amusement............... 18
4. Ministry Partnerships and Collaboration 24

Section 2: Perspectives on the Heart of a Shepherd

5. Motivation for Ministry 37
6. Humility, Brokenness, and Ministry 42
7. Passion for Ministry 47
8. Jealousy and Envy..................................... 53
9. Secret Sins of Pastors 58

Section 3: Perspectives on Nurturing the Flock

10. Expository Preaching 65
11. Priority of Prayer.................................... 73
12. Balance in Ministry.................................. 77
13. Biblical Counseling.................................. 82
14. Love, Emotional Intelligence, and People Skills............ 90

Section 4: Perspectives on Culture and Ministry

15 Defending the Faith 97
16 Forgetting the Doctrine of Separation 103
17 Responding to Cultural Decline 110
18 Blessings and Challenges of Rural Ministry 114
19 Compassion and Poverty Ministry 121

Section 5: Perspectives on Navigating Challenges

20 Success and Discouragement 129
21 Ethics in Ministry 134
22 Creativity and Change 143
23 Discernment 148
24 Attitude, Optimism, and Humor 152

Section 6: Perspectives on the Legacy of a Shepherd

25 Transitions and Successors 163
26 When They Leave Your Church 168
27 Mission Drift 176
28 Stewardship of Leadership 182
29 Resilience, Perseverance, and Endurance 186

PREFACE

This book is the culmination of over fifty years of pastoral ministry and leadership experience. Its content has been shaped by the diverse roles I've held throughout my ministry journey—youth pastor, church planter, Bible camp program director, rescue mission chaplain, Bible college professor, senior pastor. I've served as the executive director of an association of churches, a university trustee, a seminary trustee, a board member for two international mission agencies, seminary professor, and executive pastor. Each role has contributed insights to the pastoral perspectives I now share.

It's important for the reader to note that the opening chapter of this book on pastoral competencies is drawn directly from my doctoral work at The Southern Baptist Theological Seminary. Its more academic tone stands in marked contrast to the rest of the book, and it establishes the foundation for the pastoral perspectives that follow. The subsequent chapters of the book aim to instruct, motivate, challenge, encourage, and equip pastors and ministry leaders as they serve faithfully in their shepherding role. Twenty-one of the chapters were originally published as articles in *VOICE* magazine, the official publication of IFCA International that I had the privilege of editing for two decades. These chapters were originally written as stand-alone articles for my brothers in that association of churches, and they differ in length, style, and purpose. This becomes particularly noticeable when compiled in book form. Also, the citations in these chapters come from the day when the articles were written, between 1999 and 2019.

Eight chapters of this book were developed from lecture materials I originally presented in courses taught in the Pastoral Theology department at Shepherds Theological Seminary since 2019. I am grateful for this privilege I've had to train the next generation of shepherds who will lead Christ's church with wisdom and courage.

My prayer is that these collected perspectives—born from both academic study and frontline ministry experience—will serve as encouragement and a practical resource for those called to pastoral leadership in an increasingly complex world.

Many contributed to the perspectives I share in this book, and they shouldn't be overlooked. First, I must thank my precious wife, Miriam, who allowed me time away, that she can never have back, to work on this project. Miriam's faithfulness to love and serve her Lord and Savior as well as our family cannot be measured. Over all these years, I spent many hours away from her in ministry responsibilities and many more hours with her at my side in ministry. I marvel at her willingness to serve and portray Christlikeness, and I have learned so much from her insights on ministry over the course of our marriage. My love for Miriam grows ever deeper each passing year, and I can't imagine my life apart from her.

Second, I wish to express my profound gratitude to three men who have walked with me in ministry for over fifty years. Dr. Ronald Manahan of Grace College and Theological Seminary in Winona Lake, Indiana has been my academic and personal mentor for these five decades, and his pursuit of wisdom, truth, holiness, and love over all these years has been a shining example to me. Ronald Thompson of Frontier School of the Bible in LaGrange, Wyoming has been mentoring me in pastoral ministry ever since I was twenty years old, and our lifelong relationship has blessedly informed my philosophy of pastoral ministry. Chris Bauer in Santa Rosa, California has been my beloved and closest friend and wise personal advisor ever since God presented him to me as my college roommate, which is amazing since we also grew up living two blocks away from each other in Winona, Minnesota. These three men have shaped my life profoundly, each leaving an indelible imprint on my character and ministry philosophy, and their wisdom, example, and timely guidance have transformed how I understand my calling and how I've navigated the complexities of ministry and life.

Third, I owe an immeasurable debt of gratitude to the countless ministry partners whose encouragement and support have sustained me throughout my years of service. I must offer special thanksgiving to God for the profound influence of Ira Ransom, Ray Ransom, Bob Graves, and Jerry Smith—faithful servants who now rejoice in the presence of the Lord. Their wise and godly examples continue to inspire me even in their absence.

Preface

The men with whom I served on the boards of IFCA International, Biblical Ministries Worldwide, Calvary University, and Shepherds Theological Seminary each contributed uniquely to my personal and pastoral development. Among these many colleagues, too numerous to list here, Roy Sprague, Paul Seger, Bob Provost, Dan Fredericks, Earl Brubaker, and Tom Zobrist became treasured co-laborers. Their wisdom, instruction, and friendship have been invaluable gifts along this journey.

The congregations I've been blessed to serve as pastor in Utah, Michigan, Indiana, and North Carolina have been filled with remarkable people who have deeply enriched me and my understanding of what it means to be a local church shepherd. Many of the leaders and members of these churches continue to bless me today through wonderful friendship and fellowship; these lasting relationships remain among the most treasured of my ministry years.

In these more recent years, my ministry at The Shepherd's Church has been enriched beyond measure through my Senior Pastor Stephen Davey and my brothers Jimmy Carter and Kevin Welch. These three men have served as trusted confidants, wise counselors, and faithful friends who've walked alongside me through both triumphs and trials. They exemplify the covenant brotherhood described in Proverbs 17:17.

Fourth, I leaned heavily on the wisdom and support of many members of the academic community. In my early academic ministry, the faculty of Grand Rapids School of Bible and Music and then the faculty and administration of Grace Theological Seminary were there for wise counsel and loving support. In the last six years, I've grown to love all the men on the faculty of Shepherds Theological Seminary. But Tim Sigler, Thomas Pittman, and Andrew Burggraff were especially generous with their time and expert counsel to help push me through my doctoral studies, and Tim Miller expertly advised me regarding publishing this book. Throughout my doctoral work at SBTS, Dr. Justin Irving was there as my supervisor, advisor, and friend. I grew to love Justin, and I'm thankful that in God's sweet providence he was my faculty supervisor. Men from other educational institutions assisted me in my doctoral pursuit as well. Appalachian Bible College administrator and professor, and then later Marshall University professor, Dr. Charles Bethel along with Grace Theological Seminary professor Dr. Rock LaGioia gave me great support at crucial times in my work, and I am thankful for them.

Lastly, my family has been the wellspring of strength throughout my ministry. My children, their spouses, and the grandsons they've presented to Miriam and me have brought immeasurable joy to our home. The laughter, love, and simple moments we've shared as a family have sustained me during countless seasons of ministry fatigue. When the work of shepherding left me depleted, returning to them at home consistently restored my spirit and reminded me of life's deepest blessings. My prayer is that all of us will follow The Lofquist Family Code, which has officially been ours for thirty years: Walk with Wisdom. Stand for Holiness. Live for Christ.

The above demonstrates that achievements in ministry are never accomplished alone. As I have written inside this book, ministry is about partnerships, collaboration, cooperation, networking, interdependence, sharing, teamwork, and working together. My pastoral ministry gives evidence of this truth, and I'm profoundly grateful to God for my family, friends, and ministry partners.

Les Lofquist
Cary, North Carolina
July 2025

PERSPECTIVES ON PASTORAL LEADERSHIP

1
A Biblical Theology of Leadership

WHAT DOES A GODLY and effective leader look like? How does he think, and what motivates him? Most importantly, what is a biblical theology of leadership, and how does that inform a philosophy of leadership?

The thesis of this chapter is that a biblical theology of leadership begins with Christ, involves others in purposeful, cooperative activity, and ultimately aims to cultivate a biblical foundation for the church or organization. This idea will be developed by defining leadership and examining four key biblical examples that shape a theology of leadership rooted in Scripture.

A Definition of Leadership

Some define leadership in just one word: "To put it simply, leadership is influence."[1] Others prefer a popular definition that has been around for many years: "leadership ... is the art or science of getting things done through people."[2] Another defines leadership as "the capacity and will to rally men and women to a common purpose, and the character which inspires confidence."[3] There are many definitions of leadership in both the secular and Christian world.

A detailed definition of Christian, spiritual leadership is that of Wilder and Jones: "The Christ-following leader—living as a bearer of God's image in union with Christ—develops a diverse community of fellow laborers who are equipped and empowered to pur-

---

[1] John MacArthur, *Called to Lead: 26 Leadership Lessons from the Life of the Apostle Paul* (Nashville: Thomas Nelson, 2004), vi.

[2] Ted Engstrom, *The Making of a Christian Leader* (Grand Rapids: Zondervan, 1976), 138.

[3] J. Oswald Sanders, *Spiritual Leadership*, (Chicago: Moody Publishers, 2007), 29.

sue shared goals that fulfill the creation mandate and the Great Commission in submission to the Word of God."[4] This definition of leadership begins with Christ, who is the proper starting point for biblical leadership.

The leader is first to be a Christ-follower who is living in vital communion with Christ. Ultimately, the leader should involve other people in purposeful activity, and this activity should be focused on fortifying a biblical foundation for the organization with the goal of gospel advance. But to have "effective, compelling vision for ministry, the kind of vision that will motivate people to follow, the Christian leader must have a deep and intimate walk with Christ and listen to and be filled with the Holy Spirit."[5] Cochrum notes, "Leadership is influence. Spiritual leadership is spiritual influence."[6] And spiritual influence begins with Christ.

Key Biblical References to Leadership

Romans 12:8 teaches that "one who leads" does so because of a spiritual gift from God. 1 Corinthians 12:28 refers to the spiritual gift of administration, using the Greek word *kubernēseis* that literally refers to the skill with which a pilot guides a ship, or the helmsman who was the responsible decision-maker on a ship.[7] The church at Thessalonica was commanded to "recognize those who labor among you, and are over you in the Lord and admonish you" (1Thess 5:12). This is a clear statement that there were those "over" the church in Thessalonica (same word as translated "rule" in 1 Tim 5:17). And Hebrews 13:17 says, "Obey those who rule over you, and be submissive, for they watch out for your souls, as those who must give account." The fact of human leadership is clearly demonstrated in the Bible and expected in practice.

Jesus laid down the ultimate principle regarding leadership when he said, "For even the Son of Man came not to be served but to serve, and to give his life as a ransom for many" (Mark 10:45). His command that the greatest should serve others is absolutely contrary to the understanding of

---

4 Michael S. Wilder and Timothy Paul Jones, *The God Who Goes Before You* (Nashville: Broadman & Holman, 2018), 16.

5 Sherwood G. Lingenfelter, *Leading Cross-Culturally* (Grand Rapids: Baker Academic, 2008), 32.

6 Ken Cochrum, *Close: Leading Well Across Distance and Cultures* (Create Space, 2013), 163.

7 Timothy Friberg, Barbara Friberg, and Neva F. Miller, *Analytical Lexicon of the Greek New Testament* (Grand Rapids: Baker, 2000), 239.

leadership in the world (see Mark 10:42–44). His example of humble servanthood when he washed the feet of the disciples (John 13:1–17) demonstrates the biblical paradigm about leadership: "greatness comes through servanthood, and leadership through becoming a slave of all."[8]

Stacy makes this conclusion: "In the New Testament, 'leadership' is a matter of *guiding* rather than *governing*."[9] New Testament leading is not about aggressive driving and pushing, but about leading as a shepherd leads, in front of the sheep.[10]

Key Biblical Examples of Leadership

Examining Scripture for examples of leadership is useful to inform a biblical theology of leadership. The Bible is filled with examples of leaders—some good, many bad—but there are four key biblical examples whose lives and ministries are most helpful in shaping a biblical theology of leadership.

Moses

Born to a Hebrew mother but raised in Pharaoh's palace, "Moses was educated in all the wisdom of the Egyptians and was powerful in speech and action" (Acts 7:22). Forced to flee to the desert of Midian at age forty (Exod 2:15), Moses remained in the desert until the age of eighty (Exod 7:7). Those forty years of obscurity became the crucible in which God prepared Moses to lead over two million people out of Egypt.[11] It is staggering to consider one man in that kind of leadership position.

Moses demonstrated a number of characteristics that are instructive for developing a theology of leadership. Some of these include: steadfastness in crisis (Exod 12:1–15:21), patience in the face of intense criticism and grumbling (Exod 15:22–17:15), wisdom in delegation (Exod 18:1–27), intercessor for a rebellious people (Exod 32:1–33:6), intimacy with God (Exod 33:7–34:35), skillful organizer of a large-scale project [the tabernacle] (Exod 35:4–40:38), guardian of holiness (Lev 10:1–7), crisis intervention (Num

---

8 J. Oswald Sanders, *Spiritual Leadership* (Chicago: Moody, 2007), 24.

9 Robert Wayne Stacy, "A Concept Study: Leadership in New Testament Greek," in *Biblical Leadership*, edited by Benjamin K. Forrest and Chet Roden (Grand Rapids: Kregel Academic, 2017), 303.

10 Timothy S. Laniak, *Shepherds after My Own Heart*, 54.

11 This number is derived from Numbers 1:17–46, where 600,000 men are included in the census. Extrapolating that number to include women and children, the total can be fairly estimated to exceed two million.

13:1–14:45), withstanding a frontal attack (Num 16:1–50), and preparing his successor (Num 27:12–23, Deut 31:1–34:12).[12]

The assessment of Moses in Deuteronomy 34:10–12 demonstrates that he is the greatest of leaders, worthy of emulation.

> And there has not arisen a prophet since in Israel like Moses, whom the LORD knew face to face, none like him for all the signs and the wonders that the LORD sent him to do in the land of Egypt, to Pharaoh and to all his servants and to all his land, and for all the mighty power and all the great deeds of terror that Moses did.

Traditionally in Judaism, Moses is considered the greatest prophet of all.[13] His example of greatness is truly instructive for leadership, but his example of humility is even more inspiring: "Moses was very meek, more than all people who were on the face of the earth." (Num 12:3).

Nehemiah

Nehemiah was the political leader of the post-Exilic community in Israel, returning from the Persian capital Susa to Jerusalem upon hearing of the dire circumstances in Israel. In Nehemiah 1, he is introduced as the Persian king's cupbearer, which was a position of great responsibility. Royal cupbearers were not only there to protect the king from poisoning, but they "were also expected to be convivial and tactful companions to the king. Being much in his confidence, they could thus wield considerable influence by way of informal counsel and discussion."[14] This meant he would have been trained in royal etiquette, and he was "one who could well determine who got to see the king."[15] Despite all his natural abilities and status, Scripture gives the reason for Nehemiah's leadership effectiveness: "the hand of the Lord his God was on him" (Neh 1:10; 2:8, 18).

Nehemiah demonstrated a number of characteristics that are instructive for developing a theology of leadership. Nehemiah was a man of responsibil-

---

12 Don N. Howell, *Servants of the Servant* (Eugene, OR: Wipf & Stock, 2003), 29–37.

13 This is the assessment of the great Rabbi Maimonides as cited by Arthur J. Wolak, *Religion and Contemporary Management: Moses as a Model for Effective Leadership* (London: Anthem, 2016), 13.

14 H.G.M. Williamson, *Ezra, Nehemiah*, WBC (Waco, TX: Word, 1985), 174.

15 Edwin M. Yamauchi, "A Model Leader: Leadership in Nehemiah," in *Biblical Leadership*, edited by Benjamin K. Forrest and Chet Roden (Grand Rapids: Kregel Academic, 2017), 268.

ity (Neh 1:11), a man of prayer (Neh 1:4–11; 2:4–5), a man who was rightly motivated (Neh 13:14, 22, 29, 31), a man of vision (Neh 1:3; 2:13–16; 4:10), a man of action and cooperation (Neh 2:16–18; 3:1–32; 6:15; 8:9; 12:26, 36; 10:1), a man of compassion (Neh 5:2–18), and a man who triumphed over opposition (Neh 4:3; 6:5–7, 10–14).[16]

Nehemiah "mobilizes an entire community into sections to rebuild the city walls, aggressively defends the workers from threats of violence, and galvanizes the tiring workers to complete what they began. At every step he is a full participant in the project, from stone mason to night guard to water carrier."[17] Nehemiah's leadership example provides a great model to consider when developing a biblical theology of leadership.

Paul

Paul has a unique place of leadership in the history of the church, and as such, he has much to contribute toward a biblical theology of leadership. Throughout his ministry, Paul placed great importance on plurality in leadership. The size of his ministry team was quite large—Paul mentions ninety names in the New Testament.[18] He emphasized a plurality of leaders in the local church (Acts 14:23; 20:17; Titus 1:5).

His was a relational style of leadership: "we should embrace the general contours of Paul's relational style of leadership as normative for Christian leaders in every place and time."[19] Also, Paul's leadership could be generally characterized as authoritative, exhortational, accountable, affirmatory, sacrificial, and missional.[20]

One of Paul's great contributions to formulating a biblical theology of leadership is in regards to mentoring. He commanded Timothy in 2 Timothy 2:2, "what you have heard from me in the presence of many witnesses entrust to faithful men who will be able to teach others also." With this command as the backdrop, carefully observe Paul's approach to mentoring Timothy. "This approach includes carefully selecting and training as the right person for the job, equipping him for the tasks of ministry, empowering him

---

16 Yamauchi, "A Model Leader: Leadership in Nehemiah," 267–274.

17 Howell, *Servants of the Servant*, 127.

18 Felix lists these names in "Paul's Associates and Co-Workers," https://catholic-resources.org/Bible/PaulineAssociates.htm.

19 Joseph H. Hellerman, "Community and Relationships: Leadership in Pauline Theology," in *Biblical Leadership*, edited by Benjamin K. Forrest and Chet Roden (Grand Rapids: Kregel Academic, 2017), 430.

20 Howell, *Servants of the Servant*, 256–282.

for success, employing him for effectiveness, and communicating the value of their relationship."[21]

Based on a study of Paul's leadership in the shipwreck of Acts 27 and his relationship with the Corinthian church as seen in 1 Corinthians, MacArthur has determined twenty-six characteristics of a true leader.[22] Nine of these specific characteristics that MacArthur identifies are especially helpful in informing a biblical theology of leadership: (1) a leader is trustworthy, (2) takes the initiative, (3) uses good judgment, (4) is optimistic, (5) empowers by example, (6) is decisive, (7) knows when to change his mind, (8) is courageous, (9) is disciplined. Paul provides a great example of leadership for the church and the secular world.

Jesus

The example of Jesus is the supreme model for leadership: "Christian leadership models itself upon our Lord Jesus Christ. . . . We are spiritually effective as leaders when we follow His example."[23] However, there is one very important admonition from Stetzer when studying the Lord Jesus in light of leadership principles: "Jesus did not come to be your leadership guru. He came to die on the cross, for your sin, and in your place. Yet, he did lead. And we can learn from how he led."[24]

The principles that Stetzer notes are instructive for informing a biblical theology of leadership. Six of Stetzer's principles observe that Jesus: (1) humbled himself and allowed God to exalt him (Phil 2:5–11), (2) followed his Father's will rather than seeking a position (John 6:38; 4:34), (3) defined greatness as being a servant (Mark 9:33–37), (4) left his place at the head table to serve the needs of others (John 13:4–5), (5) shared responsibility and authority with those he loved (Luke 9:1–2), (6) built a team to carry out a vision worldwide (Matt 28:18–20).[25]

---

21 Stacey E. Hoehl, "The Mentor Relationship: An Exploration of Paul as Loving Mentor to Timothy and the Application of the Relationship to Contemporary Leadership Challenges," *Journal of Biblical Perspectives in Leadership* 3, no. 2 (Summer 2011): 35.

22 John MacArthur, *Called to Lead: 26 Leadership Lessons from the Life of the Apostle Paul* (Nashville: Thomas Nelson, 2004), 209.

23 Derek Prime and Alistair Begg, *On Being a Pastor* (Chicago: Moody, 2004), 219.

24 Ed Stetzer, "7 Principles to Lead As Jesus Led," *Christianity Today Blog*, 27 September 2017, https://www.christianitytoday.com/edstetzer/2017/september/7-principles-to-lead-as-jesus-led.html.

25 Stetzer, "7 Principles to Lead as Jesus Led."

In another study of Jesus as a model for leadership, Sloan draws some important considerations based on the ministry of Christ. Eight of his considerations note that Jesus: (1) spoke knowledgeably, (2) was a teacher who gathered around himself concentric circles of learners, (3) corrected clearly, quickly, and impartially, (4) used both public and common settings for his teachings, (5) had a strong devotional life, (6) had a shrewdness that he practiced and commended, (7) commended God-honoring risk taking, (8) profoundly honored the truth both in living and in speaking.[26] Christian leaders must carefully study Jesus' ministry to inform their biblical theology of leadership. He is our perfect example of a leader.

Defining leadership and examining four key examples of biblical leadership help in describing biblical leadership. All of these elements lay the foundation for the concept of a biblical theology of leadership.

---

26 Robert B. Sloan, "A Biblical Model of Leadership," in *Christian Leadership Essentials*, edited by David S. Dockery (Nashville: Broadman & Holman Academic, 2011), 13–21.

2

Components for a Philosophy of Leadership

EVERY EFFECTIVE CHRISTIAN LEADER operates from a philosophy of leadership, whether articulated or not, that shapes his decisions and interactions. A personal philosophy of leadership is essential for every pastor or ministry leader as it provides a foundation for daily leadership decisions and practices. When developed intentionally, this philosophy becomes an internal compass that guides a leader through both routine situations and complex challenges.

This chapter presents a checklist of twelve essential components that comprise a biblical philosophy of leadership. Each component represents a critical aspect of leadership that, when embraced and implemented, leads to greater ministry effectiveness and spiritual impact. These twelve components create a comprehensive framework for leadership that honors God while serving people with wisdom.

Following Christ

The single most crucial element of a personal philosophy of Christian leadership is that the leader must first be a follower of Jesus Christ. As Wilder and Jones explain, "We are not called to lead like Jesus in the sense of attempting to imitate his precise practices of management or administration; instead, we are called to lead as followers of Jesus. In fact, in one sense, the people we lead should not be following us at all."[27] The Christian leader should first and foremost be a humble, obedient Christ-follower: "He is a leader *because* he

---

27 Michael S. Wilder and Timothy Paul Jones, *The God Who Goes before You* (Nashville: Broadman & Holman, 2018), 21.

is a follower."[28] Leaders who attempt to forge their own path without first following Christ will inevitably lead others astray.

This priority of following Christ is modeled by the apostle Paul who said, "Follow me as I follow Christ" (1 Cor 11:1). Paul's leadership was effective precisely because his primary allegiance was to Christ. Contemporary Christian leadership must maintain this same foundation—being first and foremost followers before attempting to lead others.

Character / Modeling

Spiritual character must form the foundation of a leader's ministry before the question of leadership competencies arises. Competencies and abilities, which refer to observable outward actions, differ from the qualities that refer to inward character traits that should ultimately define the leader. Newton wrote this in regard to the essential qualities that must be present in an elder: "Without exaggerating, character is everything when it comes to the pastor/elder."[29] Without godly character and humility, leadership competencies mean nothing in biblical leadership. As Newton further asserts, "No amount of oratorical, leadership, or administrative skills can compensate for a lack of godly character."[30] Leadership can't be reduced to abilities and influence without the foundation of character, because leadership involves modeling an example to others. Leaders don't just use words in their communication, they communicate (for better or worse) through their actions.[31]

The qualifications for elders in 1 Timothy 3:1–7 and Titus 1:5–9 emphasize character over competence. While competence is important, the overwhelming emphasis falls on the leader's moral and ethical character. This emphasis is not accidental; it reveals God's priority in leadership. The pastor-leader demonstrates in daily living what it means to follow Christ in every aspect of life.

---

28 Timothy S. Laniak, *Shepherds after My Own Heart* (Downers Grove, IL: IVP Press, 2006), 22.

29 Phil A. Newton, *40 Questions about Pastoral Ministry* (Grand Rapids: Kregel Academic, 2021), 37.

30 Newton, *40 Questions about Pastoral Ministry*, 37.

31 Justin A. Irving and Mark L. Strauss, *Leadership in Christian Perspective* (Grand Rapids: Baker Academic, 2019), 17–18.

Giftedness

Romans 12:8 teaches that "one who leads" does so because of a spiritual gift from God. First Corinthians 12:28 refers to the spiritual gift of administration, using the Greek word *kubernēseis* that literally refers to the skill with which a pilot guides a ship, or the helmsman who was the responsible decision-maker on a ship.[32] While all believers have spiritual gifts, some "have a specialized gift to focus, harmonize and coordinate the giftedness of other believers."[33] This gifting of the Spirit is an important consideration in biblical leadership, but giftedness comes from God alone, not from human effort or natural ability.

While natural talents should be developed and refined, spiritual leadership ultimately flows from spiritual gifting. Leaders must recognize their specific gifts, develop them appropriately, and use them with wisdom for the church's ultimate benefit.

Servanthood

Jesus laid down the ultimate principle regarding leadership when he said, "For even the Son of Man came not to be served but to serve, and to give his life as a ransom for many" (Mark 10:45). His command that the greatest should serve others is contrary to the understanding of leadership in the world (see Mark 10:42–44). His example of humble servanthood, when he washed the feet of the disciples (John 13:1–17), demonstrates the biblical paradigm about leadership: "greatness comes through servanthood, and leadership through becoming a slave of all."[34]

Jesus modeled radical and sacrificial servanthood. This type of leadership rejects authority from position or title as the primary basis for leadership influence. Instead, a servant embraces sacrifice, humility, and concern for others' well-being as the foundation for genuine influence. Servant leaders value people's growth and development above their own advancement. They measure success not by personal accomplishments but by the spiritual success of those they lead.

---

32 Timothy Friberg, Barbara Friberg, and Neva F. Miller, *Analytical Lexicon of the Greek New Testament* (Grand Rapids: Baker, 2000), 239.

33 James E. Plueddemann, *Leading Across Cultures* (Downers Grove, IL: IVP Academic, 2009), 173.

34 J. Oswald Sanders, *Spiritual Leadership* (Chicago: Moody, 2007), 24.

Collaboration

Noting the importance of collaboration to the apostle Paul, Irving and Strauss state, "Paul was all about relationship, collaboration, and partnership."[35] This collaborative work arises from a shared vision, it encourages humility and the valuing of giftedness, it results in greater effectiveness, and it produces a greater sense of community.[36] Leaders are called to "create environments that are conducive to high levels of personal motivation, resulting in increased effectiveness and joy among followers."[37] No Christian leader should ever seek tyrannical power over others. Biblical leadership is not based on "commands and demands," but it's exercised in a genuinely collaborative manner.

The most effective church leaders recognize that no single person possesses all the wisdom, insight, or abilities needed for effective ministry. By creating collaborative teams, leaders multiply their effectiveness while simultaneously developing future leaders. Team-based ministry also provides accountability, prevents burnout, and models the body of Christ in action.

Stewardship

All leaders have been entrusted by God to serve, and they serve under God's ultimate authority. One day they must give an accounting for their leadership. This means that leadership is a stewardship from God:

> The biblical concept of a steward is simple. A steward is someone who manages and leads what is not his own, and he leads knowing that he will give an account to the Lord as the owner and ruler of all. Stewards are entrusted with responsibility. . . . Christian leaders are invested [by God] with a stewardship of influence, authority, and trust that we are called to fulfill.[38]

Leadership is not for the benefit of the leader, but for the benefit of the people, to the glory of God, and under the accountability of God.

Stewardship extends to every aspect of leadership. Leaders are stewards of the gospel message, ensuring its faithful transmission (1 Cor 4:1–2). They are stewards of people's spiritual well-being (Heb 13:17). They are stewards

---

35 Irving and Strauss, *Leadership in Christian Perspective*, 56.

36 Irving and Strauss, *Leadership in Christian Perspective*, 58–60.

37 Wilder and Jones, *The God Who Goes before You*, 18.

38 Albert Mohler, *The Conviction to Lead*, (Minneapolis: Bethany House, 2012), 135–136.

of organizational resources, both material and human. They are stewards of influence, using their platforms responsibly. They are stewards of time, managing priorities to focus on what matters most. Biblical stewardship demands both faithfulness and fruitfulness. Leadership positions are not possessions to be grasped but trusts to be managed.

Authority in Balance with Love

Leaders must set the climate of love in their organization. They are called to "create environments that are conducive to high levels of personal motivation, resulting in increased effectiveness and joy among followers."[39] In contrast, Napoleon is quoted as saying, "I like only those people who are useful to me, and only so long as they are useful."[40] Some leaders follow Napoleon's philosophy of leadership, using people to build up their own reputation and bring glory to themselves as they seek to expand their own little empire. Napoleon was a tyrant who sought personal fame and glory through power. No Christian leader should ever seek tyrannical power over others for his own glory. Biblical leadership is not on a "command and demand" basis. But loving leadership is administered by example and godly character, with moral leadership and respect that is earned through a pattern of good judgment.

The proper use of authority remains one of the most challenging aspects of Christian leadership. Scripture recognizes legitimate authority in leadership positions (Rom 13:1–7, Heb 13:17), but this authority must always be exercised through love. Authority without love becomes tyrannical; love without appropriate authority becomes ineffective. Paul's leadership provides an instructive model. In Philemon, he could command but preferred to appeal (Phlm 8–9). And as Peter writes, pastors should lead "not domineering over those in your charge, but being examples to the flock" (1 Pet 5:3).

Vision

Leadership is seeing a goal more clearly than others and inspiring them to pursue the goal with you. The leader must be able to see farther and more clearly than those he leads, and visionary leadership is a critical element for a pastor or ministry leader.[41] Poor leaders often feel overwhelmed by events

---

39 Wilder and Jones, *The God Who Goes before You*, 18.

40 J. Christopher Herold, ed. and trans., *The Mind of Napoleon: A Selection of His Written and Spoken Words* (New York City: Columbia University Press, 1955), 9.

41 Bob R. Agee, "Leadership, Vision, and Strategic Planning," in *Christian Leadership Essentials*, ed. David S. Dockery (Nashville: Broadman & Holman Academic, 2011), 48.

and their own inabilities, and then they drift along with no clear vision for the future. Effective leaders focus on future goals and look for ways to accomplish them.

Biblical vision is always anchored in God's revealed purposes. Unlike secular vision that may originate from personal ambition or organizational needs, Christian leadership vision flows from understanding God's will as revealed in Scripture. When leaders cast compelling biblical vision, they provide focus, motivation, and direction. Vision unites diverse individuals around common purpose and prevents the distractions of lesser priorities.

Strategy / Intentionality

The leader must relentlessly pursue purposeful, visionary planning and forethought in order to determine and achieve goals for himself and for his organization. Intentionality is crucial for leaders, and intentionality begins with vision, followed by initial assessment and planning, which leads to a linkage of strategy to operations and processes.[42] Geiger and Peck make the observation that to produce leaders, it takes three elements: a strong conviction to develop leaders, a healthy culture for leadership development, and helpful constructs, systems, processes, and programs.[43] In addition, implementation becomes essential for leaders: "Unless you translate big thoughts into concrete steps for action, they're pointless."[44]

Strategic thinking bridges vision and reality. While vision establishes the destination, strategy determines the path to reach it. Effective ministry strategy includes several essential elements: clear goals aligned with vision, resource allocation plans, measurable outcomes, timeline development, role clarification, and evaluation processes. Without intentional strategy, ministries default to maintaining existing systems and the status quo.

Openness and Acceptance

Biblical leadership demonstrates love and establishes a secure environment for those we lead. With openness and acceptance, biblical leaders set the tone in their church or ministry organization.

---

[42] Agee "Leadership, Vision, and Strategic Planning," 46–64.

[43] Eric Geiger and Kevin Peck, *Designed to Lead* (Nashville: Broadman & Holman, 2016), 14–15.

[44] Larry Bossidy and Ram Charan, *Execution: The Discipline of Getting Things Done* (New York: Crown Business, 2002), 19.

The pastor-leader should strive to create an environment in church where people feel respected, creativity is welcomed, honest feedback emerges, and genuine community develops. This environment doesn't mean an absence of accountability or biblical standards; rather, it means creating a ministry where people can serve without fear of rejection or humiliation while being taught the word of God and its holy standards.

Wartime Mentality

Tripp gives pastors an important reminder: "It is essential to understand that leadership in any gospel ministry is spiritual war."[45] Christian leaders have an active and unseen enemy, with supernatural power and an innumerable number in his evil army, and all of them are focused on destroying God's work. "No leadership community should be naïve. No leadership community should do its work with a comfortable peacetime mentality."[46] These words are a call to realism, awareness, and a condition of spiritual alertness in leadership.

Scripture consistently portrays ministry leadership as spiritual warfare. Paul describes the Christian life using military metaphors (Eph 6:10–20, 2 Tim 2:3–4) and reminds leaders that "we do not wrestle against flesh and blood, but against the rulers, against the authorities, against the cosmic powers over this present darkness" (Eph 6:12). This warfare perspective brings necessary urgency and vigilance to leadership, demanding constant vigilance against both internal and external threats to the church's spiritual health. Leaders must maintain awareness of cultural, theological, and organizational dangers that lead to compromise and mission drift.

Dialogic Communication

Leaders who are effective must be effective communicators interpersonally and corporately. "If leadership is primarily about guiding and motivating people—which it is—then communication is absolutely essential for effective leadership practice."[47] This component of biblical leadership involves shared dialogue to determine the organization's course of action as opposed to monologic communication, which refers to giving information to others without shared discussion. Pastors who care about the success of their

---

45 Paul David Tripp, *Lead: 12 Gospel Principles for Leadership in the Church.* (Wheaton, IL: Crossway, 2020), 114.

46 Tripp, *Lead,* 121.

47 Irving and Strauss, *Leadership in Christian Perspective,* 141.

church must also care about authentic listening.[48] Others in the organization have valuable perspective and insight and need to be heard by the leader.

Communication represents perhaps the most time-consuming activity of effective pastoral leadership. This communication takes multiple forms: preaching, teaching, vision-casting, conflict resolution, encouragement, correction, and organizational dialogue. The most effective leaders recognize that communication requires both clear expression and attentive listening. James instructs believers to be "quick to hear, slow to speak" (Jas 1:19), advice particularly pertinent to those in leadership.

Conclusion

The twelve components presented above help create a philosophy for leadership that honors God while serving people with wisdom. Having a personal philosophy of leadership is essential for every pastor or ministry leader as it provides a foundation for daily leadership decisions and practices. When developed intentionally, this philosophy will guide a leader through both routine situations and complex challenges.

A biblical philosophy of leadership could be summarized this way: "When a leader focuses on the common good, delegates responsibility and power to others, and employs the power of dialogue and effective communications, that leader motivates and enables a team to achieve its maximum potential and results."[49]

---

48   Irving and Strauss, *Leadership in Christian Perspective*, 158.

49   Sherwood G. Lingenfelter, *Leading Cross-Culturally* (Grand Rapids: Baker Academic, 2008), 147.

3

Serious Ministry in a World of Amusement

Several decades ago, Annie Dillard posed a profound question: "Why do people in churches seem like cheerful, brainless tourists on a packaged tour of the Absolute?"[50] Do you think such an assessment could be made today?

We live in an entertainment saturated society. And the danger of living in such a society is to prefer a more fun-filled deity, trivializing the one true God and minimizing his holy standards, happily entertaining ourselves with illusions of Christianity. Minimal sense of awe, little reverence, lots of laughs. The problem is that all of this is so corrupt and unbiblical. Soon (and quite predictably) the punch lines start to grow old, smiles are replaced by yawns, and yawns lead to carelessness, heresy, and moral defection.

The New Testament warns us to "offer to God acceptable worship, with reverence and awe, for our God is a consuming fire" (Heb 12:28–29). It seems all too often that talk of the consuming fire of the Lord God Almighty gets extinguished by entertaining, happy god-talk.

Gimmicks, fads, and feel-good faith are replacing the real thing in the lives of all too many Christians. Knowing Christ and his Word has been replaced by the notion that ministries must be based on philosophies that are entertaining or therapeutic. The solid foundation of truth has been often obscured by the bright lights of the stage and overlooked for style, image, and hype. The end result is that we've fallen prey to the insights and mindset of the world of entertainment, swallowing powerful myths such as the desperate need for fun and relevance-at-any-cost.

---

50 Annie Dillard, *Teaching a Stone to Talk* (New York: Harper & Row, 1982), 40.

We need a clear understanding of who we are, where we live, and where we're headed.

Christians and the World

Christ said that his disciples are "not of this world" (John 17:14). Peter wrote that we are "aliens and strangers" (1 Pet 2:11). Paul wrote that "our citizenship is in heaven" (Phil 3:20). The Bible is clear. Those who are Christ's are citizens of another kingdom, one which is invisible to human eyes and can't be reached by man-made transportation.

The Greek word for world (*kosmos*) originally meant an ordered system[51] and reflects the orderliness of the world as viewed by the ancient Greeks. It referred to the world in its most inclusive sense, the ordered planet on which we live: "The God who made the *kosmos* and everything in it, being Lord of heaven and earth, does not live in temples made by man" (Acts 17:24).

The word *kosmos* also refers to the world of humanity in general. It is used this way in John 3:16 ("God so loved the *kosmos*"). It was also used this way in 1 John 2:2 ("He is the propitiation for our sins, and not for ours only but also for the sins of the whole *kosmos*").

Also, *kosmos* is often used to refer to that which is organized against God and is hostile to him, lost in sin, ruined, depraved. It is used this way six times in John 15:18–19 ("If the *kosmos* hates you, know that it has hated me before it hated you. If you were of the *kosmos*, the *kosmos* would love you as its own; but because you are not of the *kosmos*, but I chose you out of the *kosmos*, therefore the *kosmos* hates you"). It's also used this way in John 16:33, John 17:14 (Christ's disciples "are not of this *kosmos*"), 1 Corinthians 3:19, and 1 John 2:15 ("Do not love the *kosmos* or the things in the *kosmos*. If anyone loves the *kosmos*, the love of the Father is not in him"). And according to Christ, Satan is "the prince of this *kosmos*" (John 12:31, 16:11).

When you summarize the New Testament usage of *kosmos*, you see the following meanings:

- The planet earth (Acts 17:25)
- The orderly adornment of hair, clothing (1 Pet 3:3)
- Humanity in general (John 3:16, 1 John 2:2)

---

51 F. Wilbur Gingrich, Walter Bauer, and William Arndt, *Shorter Lexicon of the Greek New Testament* (Chicago: University of Chicago Press, 1965), 112.

- The organized world system that hates God and is hostile toward him (John 17:14, 1 John 2:15–16)

Regarding how Christians should relate to the *kosmos*, the last two bullet points above are most instructive. Because God loves humanity in general and Christ died for all humanity (He is the atoning sacrifice for our sins and those of all humanity), we too should love people as God does and share the gospel so they can place their faith in Christ's atoning sacrifice. But we shouldn't love the organized world system that openly hates God and is in open hostility against him. Love people. Don't love the world's system.

Christians and This Present Age

There is another important word in the New Testament related to our discussion, and that is the Greek word *aiōn* from which we get the English word eon. This word can mean "a very long time ago" or "ages past" (regarding holy prophets of old in Luke 1:70 and the beginning of time when the world began in John 9:32).

It also means "eternity in the future, forevermore" (regarding eternal life through Christ in John 6:51 and the eternal torment of the beast and false prophet in Revelation 20:10) as well as the eternal aspect of God's person (Rom 16:27), the eternal glory of Jesus Christ (Heb 13:21).

Another way the word *aiōn* is used in the New Testament is the material universe created by Jesus Christ (Heb 1:2).

The final way the word *aiōn* is used in the New Testament is regarding the future joyful age (Mark 10:30; Eph 1:21) and the present evil age (Gal 1:4) where there are worries (Matt 13:22), shrewd people (Luke 16:8), where Satan blinds the unbelievers (2 Cor 4:4), and where Satan is a prince (Eph 2:2).

When you summarize the New Testament usage of *aiōn*, you see the following meanings:

- A very long time ago or ages past (Luke 1:70, John 9:32)
- Eternity in the future (John 6:51, Rev 20:10)
- The eternal nature of God (Rom 16:27, Heb 13:21)
- The material universe created by Jesus Christ (Heb 1:2)
- The future joyful age (Mark 10:30, Eph 1:21)
- The present evil age where Satan is prince (Gal 1:4, 2 Cor 4:4, Eph 2:2)

Regarding how Christians should relate to this *aiōn*, the last two bullet points are key. Christians should remember our hope is found in the future age to come, not in this present evil age. Satan has some sort of spiritual rule in this present age as an evil prince. Because of this, we better not be deceived in this present age (as the unbelievers are, who are blinded by Satan).

Dangers for Christians

As you compare the usage of both *kosmos* and *aiōn*, you see Satan's fingerprints on both. He is a supernaturally evil prince with wicked spiritual authority over this world. He has organized this world's system in direct hostility against all things holy, in opposition to God. Plus this wicked one has an army of invisible minions who also have supernatural power to do the will of their evil ruler. Furthermore, unbelievers are completely enslaved and controlled by the flesh, and we believers have the residual influence of the flesh.

These reasons alone should give the follower of Jesus Christ a sober attitude regarding his life in this world! This world is dangerous for Christians. We need to beware of the accumulation of thoughts, opinions, speculations, impulses, and aims which are present at any time in the world because there is an evil force organized behind so many of them.

Yes, we have a regenerated nature. Yes, we have the supernatural power of the indwelling Holy Spirit. Yes, we have the Sword of the Spirit (the Word of God). Yes, we have direct access to the throne of the Lord of the universe. But the devil and his wicked army want to squeeze Christians into the mold of the world he has organized, and our flesh craves (demands!) that we go along in full agreement. That is sobering.

We live in an immoral, unholy world system. And the messages of this world, the communications of this age, are carried forth often by seemingly innocuous means mingled in with other overtly perverse means: print media, electronic media, news media, advertising, and entertainment. We are surrounded by entertainment.

If the Christian is going to live in the manner God calls him to live in this present world, he must do so in a world of amusement. And often (but most definitely *not always*) the amusing activities of the world system are energized by our adversary the devil. We must be balanced, careful not to adopt the angry attitudes of some of our fundamentalist forefathers. But like them, we must beware, ever vigilant, constantly discerning. Because we are in the world yet not of it (John 17:13–16).

Paul, Corinth, and Rome

The New Testament book of Romans stands as one of the most profound, theologically rich writings in all of Scripture. Its tone, content, and depth reveal a seriousness that confronts both the moral decay of Roman society and the shallowness of a pleasure-driven culture. Yet, what makes this even more compelling is *where* it was written from and *to whom* it was addressed.

Written from Corinth: Infamous City of Corruption

The apostle Paul wrote Romans when he was ministering in Corinth, a city infamous in the ancient world for its moral corruption and unrestrained immorality. The Greek verb *korinthiazomai* was even coined to describe a lifestyle of debauchery and sexual excess, and it literally meant "to live like a Corinthian." It was a city where wickedness was not only practiced but also celebrated.

Surrounded by this environment of rampant sin in Corinth, Paul was moved by the Holy Spirit to send a message not of compromise or casual acceptance, but of serious clarity and conviction. The city of Corinth is an important reminder that serious ministry rises out of serious darkness.

Addressed to Rome: The Entertainment Capital of the World

Paul wrote to the believers in Rome, the seat of political power and cultural influence, but also the empire's hub of entertainment, spectacle, and decadence. Gladiator games, public executions, lavish feasts, and theatrical performances defined the Roman pursuit of pleasure and distraction. Much like today's world, Rome was captivated by the next big thrill, numbing the soul with amusement while ignoring the call of eternity.

In this context, Paul didn't send a shallow message to appeal to Roman tastes. Instead, he sent a powerful and serious theological treatise, a call to righteousness, justification by faith, holy living, and a vision of God's redemptive plan for all humanity. Today, we must follow Paul's example in promoting serious ministry in our own world of amusement.

Citizens of Another World

The question that Christians need to ask ourselves is how can we be in the world but not of it? How do we live with the tension of being in two ages at once, as part of this world but citizens of another world? The only answer is we must be walking faithfully with Christ, regularly consuming his holy Word, and living a life of personal and daily spiritual renewal in the context of regular fellowship with a community of the redeemed in a Bible-teaching local church. We must exercise personal revival in our daily experience through rigorous self-confrontation (1 Pet 4:17), and we must be serious about ministry in this world of amusement.

We should aspire to the kind of ministry that serves as an antidote to the poisons of Satan's alluring world system in this present age. That kind of ministry is substantive, not shallow. At the same time, it is balanced and positive, not harsh and mean-spirited. It shines light in this dark world. It offers to God our worship, with reverence and awe, because our God is a consuming fire, not a fun-filled entertainer.

We are citizens of another world. We want to bring our holy God great glory in this present age. We need to live for the world to come with eternity's values in view. We need to help our friends and neighbors place their faith in our matchless Savior so they can join us on our pilgrimage to the next age and worship and enjoy God forever.

Yes, we live in a world of amusement. And it is to this world of amusement that we are called to bring honor to Jesus Christ. With serious ministry.

4

Ministry Partnerships and Collaboration

I BELIEVE THE ACCOMPLISHMENT OF ministry is never achieved alone. Ministry is about partnerships, collaboration, cooperation, networking, interdependence, sharing, teamwork, and working together.

Paul wrote to Timothy that ministry involves training other people, who will in turn train others to train even more people (2 Tim 2:2). In Ephesians 4:11–16 we read that the gifted leaders in the local church are to equip the believers in the local church, and the equipped believers are to do the work of ministry (v. 12); accomplishing this work leads to the building up of the body of Christ (v. 16).

The word translated as "equip" in Ephesians 4:12 means to make someone completely adequate or capable for carrying out a task. God has called the church's spiritual leaders to lead and equip the people of the church, but he never called them to "do" the work of the church. The work of ministry belongs to the church, and every member is called to be an active part of the ministry of the church. Of course, this process by necessity must happen in a series of relationships.

Another proof that ministry is never achieved in isolation is the New Testament word for fellowship: *koinōnia*. By its very definition, *koinōnia* involves commonality, community, togetherness. In the New Testament, local churches demonstrated some level of cooperation and mutual help in the fulfillment of God's purposes.

One example would be the churches of Macedonia and Achaia, which gathered offerings for the saints in Jerusalem. Another example would be in Philippians 1:5, where the apostle Paul mentioned the "participation" (*koinōnia*) of those believers "in the gospel," and in Philippians 4:15 he mentioned that they supported him while he was ministering in Thessalonica. Paul, a missionary sent out by the church at Antioch, was being supported by the church in Philippi as he planted the church in Thessalonica.

These examples are two among many in the New Testament which point to the biblical precedent and historical pattern of cooperative effort. The New Testament is clear about the primacy of the local church, but this principle does not rule out cooperative effort. In fact, the above examples demonstrate voluntary participation by the churches in Antioch and Philippi in the ministry to Thessalonica. We should not, in our desire to maintain independence, forget the biblical precedent and historical pattern of cooperative effort that has been a great practical help to the spread of the gospel, the planting of churches, and encouragement in the ministry. No church exists in isolation, as if it were an island.

Paul's Key Team Members

All of us admire solo achievement, but the truth is that no one can achieve anything of eternal value as a solitary individual. A study of the apostle Paul and the people who worked with him in the New Testament gives ample proof that Paul emphasized collaborative efforts.

Barnabas was the one who introduced Saul (Paul) to the apostles (Acts 9:26–27) and later brought him from Tarsus to Antioch (Acts 11:25–26). Paul was first a teammate to Barnabas. The Jerusalem church sent Barnabas to teach and preach to the new Greek-speaking Christians in Antioch (Acts11:19–26). And then the Christians of Antioch sent Barnabas and Paul back to Jerusalem to deliver some donations for famine relief (Acts 11:27–30). When Barnabas and Paul were sent out on another mission (Acts 13:1–14:28), Barnabas was the leader, and Paul was the assistant (Acts 14:12). Barnabas and Paul both attended the Council of Jerusalem to discuss with other Christian leaders the issue of circumcision (Acts 15:1–35). But this team would divide and separate over how to handle John Mark. After Barnabas and Paul separated, Barnabas continued preaching with Mark in Cyprus (Acts 15:39).

Paul's next teammate after Barnabas became Silas. The same man named "Silas" in Acts is always called "Silvanus" in Paul's letters and in 1 Peter 5:12. Silvanus accompanied Paul and Timothy at the beginning of their missionary activity in Macedonia and Achaia (1 Thess 1:1, 2 Thess 1:1, 2 Cor 1:19, Acts 15:40–18:5).

Paul's most important teammate was Timothy. Paul called Timothy "my beloved and faithful child in the Lord," "son" (1 Cor 4:17, 1 Tim 1:2, 2 Tim 1:2), "our brother" (1 Thess 3:2, 2 Cor 1:1, Col 1:1, Phlm 1), "a servant of Christ Jesus" (Phil 1:1), and "our/my co-worker" (1 Thess 3:2, Rom 16:21). Timothy became John Mark's replacement (Acts 16:1–5).

It seems that perhaps Paul's second-most important teammate was Titus. Paul called Titus a "son" in Titus 1:4. He told the Corinthians that Titus was "my brother" (2 Cor 2:13) and "my partner and co-worker for you" (2 Cor 8:23). The word Paul used regarding Titus that is translated "partner" is *koinōnos*, also used by Paul regarding Philemon (Phlm 17).

Paul's Other Coworkers

Paul used the term *synergoi* (literally "coworkers") mostly for his missionary coworkers. Fifteen individuals were called *synergoi* by Paul, including Prisca and Aquila (Rom 16:3), Urbanus (Rom 16:9), Timothy (Rom 16:21, 1 Thess 3:2), Titus (2 Cor 8:23), Epaphroditus (Phil 2:25), Clement (Phil 4:3), Aristarchus, Mark, and Justus (Col 4:10–11), Philemon (Phlm 1), Mark, Aristarchus, Demas, and Luke (Phlm 24). Interestingly, Paul also referred to himself and Apollos as "coworkers" (*sunergoi*) of God in 1 Corinthians 3:9 and 2 Corinthians 1:24.

Paul used several other Greek terms containing the prefix meaning "with" to designate his co-laborers, including "fellow soldier" or literally "soldier with" for Epaphroditus (Phil 2:25) and Archippus (Phlm 2); "fellow prisoner" or literally "prisoner with" for Aristarchus (Col 4:10), Epaphras (Phlm 23), Andronicus and Junia (Rom 16:7); and "fellow slave" or literally "slave with" for Epaphras (Col 1:7) and Tychicus (Col 4:7).

We also note that Paul called some people "brothers," even though they were not his blood relatives, to stress their close mutual connection. This included Quartus (Rom 16:23), Sosthenes (1 Cor 1:1), Apollos (1 Cor 16:12), Timothy (2 Cor 1:1, Col 1:1, 1 Thess 3:2, Phlm 1), Titus (2 Cor 2:13), two anonymous companions of Titus (2 Cor 8:18, 22; 12:18), Tychicus (Eph 6:21; Col 4:7), Epaphroditus (Phil 2:25), Onesimus (Col 4:9, Phlm 16), and Philemon (Phlm 7, 20). Paul also called Phoebe "our sister" (Rom 16:1) and greeted "Apphia, the sister" (Phlm 2).

I find it most interesting to observe Paul's ministry team when they conferred in Troas (Acts 20:4–6). There were seven other men listed, from five other provincial regions, who met with Paul for seven days. If the reference to "we" in Acts 20:5 includes Luke, then this ministry retreat involved eight other men plus Paul. Interesting that it occurred in Troas, where Paul earlier received the Macedonian call (Acts 16:6–10). Did Paul return to Troas in Acts 20 for a second vision retreat? Whatever the case may be, Paul met for seven days with at least seven or eight other men, and we can be sure they carefully considered their future ministry direction as a ministry team.

Paul's Team in Alphabetical Order

The passages above inspire us regarding the need for building ministry teams as Paul did. The list below amazes us when we compile all the coworkers of Paul that are mentioned in the New Testament.[52] In alphabetical order, here they are:

> Achaicus: accompanied Fortunatus to visit Paul (1 Cor 16:17–18).
>
> Agabus: a Christian prophet from Jerusalem who also visited the Christians in Antioch (Acts 11:28 where he predicted a severe famine) and Caesarea (21:10 while Paul and his companions were staying at the house of Philip the Evangelist).
>
> Apollos: an Alexandrian Jew who became a Christian missionary, described as eloquent and knowledgeable of Scripture; he preached and interacted with some of Paul's associates in Ephesus (Acts 18:24–26), in Corinth (Acts 18:27–28; 19:1; 1 Cor 1:12; 3:4–6, 22; 4:6; 16:12), and possibly on Crete (Titus 3:13). Paul called him a "brother" (1 Cor 16:12) and referred to himself, Apollos, and Cephas/Peter collectively as "servants of Christ and stewards of God's mysteries" (1 Cor 4:1).
>
> Apphia: a woman addressed by Paul as "our sister," probably a member of the household of Philemon (Phlm 2).
>
> Aquila & Prisca (Priscilla): a married couple, Jewish Christians, natives of Pontus, who were expelled from Rome in AD 49 due to the Edict of Claudius (Acts 18:1–3). They were close coworkers of Paul's early mission in Corinth (1 Cor 16:19), then leaders of the church in Ephesus (Acts 18:18, 24–28; 2 Timothy 4:19), and later evidently back in Rome, where they were leaders of a "house-church" (Rom 16:3–5).

---

52 This list is the result of many years of personal study and was originally published in *VOICE* (92:6, Nov/Dec 2013): 7–12. Since then, a study was published in 2021 also listing these ninety names by Daniel E. Parks *Paul's Associates* (grace-ebooks.com).

Archippus: a "fellow soldier" of Paul, somehow connected with Philemon (Phlm 1:2).

Aristarchus: a Christian from Thessalonica in Macedonia, a "traveling companion" (Acts 19:29, 20:4, 27:2), "fellow prisoner" (Col 4:10), and "fellow worker" (Phlm 24) of Paul.

Artemas: Paul's messenger to Titus (Titus 3:12).

Barnabas: an early apostle and senior partner of Paul, leading Paul's first ministry team.

Barsabbas: see Joseph and Judas

Carpus: Paul left books and parchments with him at Troas and asks Timothy to retrieve them (2 Tim 4:13).

Cephas: an alternate name for the apostle Peter, with whom Paul occasionally interacted (1 Cor 1:12; 3:22; 9:5; 15:5; Gal 1:18–2:14); just like Petros in Greek, Cephas in Hebrew is simply a nickname.

Chloe's people: Christians who brought Paul news about divisions in the church at Corinth (1 Cor 1:11).

Claudia (2 Tim 4:21).

Clement: a coworker of Euodia, Syntyche, and others, of whom Paul says their "names are in the book of life" (Phil 4:3).

Crescens: Paul merely reports that he has gone to Galatia (2 Tim 4:10).

Crispus: a synagogue official in Corinth (Acts 18:8), one of the very few people that Paul personally baptized (1 Cor 1:14).

Damaris: a woman who was one of Paul's few converts in Athens (Acts 17:33).

Demas: sent greetings to the Colossians (Col 4:14) and to Philemon (Phlm 24), later deserted Paul and went to Thessalonica (2 Tim 4:9–10).

Dionysius the Areopagite: a man who was one of Paul's few converts in Athens (Acts 17:34).

Epaphras: a native of Colosse and Paul's "beloved fellow servant," who probably founded the Christian community in his hometown

(Col 1:7). Paul later conveyed Epaphras' greetings back to the Colossians, calling him a "servant of Christ Jesus" who prayed on their behalf (Col 4:12), also Paul's "fellow prisoner" (probably while in Ephesus) (Phlm 23).

Epaphroditus: delivered gifts from the Philippian Christians to Paul while he was imprisoned (probably in Ephesus); Epaphroditus became ill but later recovered (Phil 2:25–30; 4:15–18).

Erastus: the "city treasurer" of Corinth (Rom 16:23, 2 Tim 4:20), whom Paul later sent to Macedonia (Acts 19:22).

Eubulus: Paul conveyed greetings to Timothy from Eubulus, Pudens, Linus, and Claudia (2 Tim 4:21).

Eunice: the mother of Timothy who was also a Christian (2 Tim 1:5).

Euodia and Syntyche: two women whom Paul urged "to agree in the Lord," and of whom Paul said, "they have labored side by side with me [Paul] in the gospel together with Clement and the rest of my fellow workers, whose names are in the book of life" (Phil 4:2–3).

Fortunatus and Achaicus: Christians from Corinth who visited Paul in Ephesus; Paul commended them (along with Stephanas) to the community, saying they have "refreshed my spirit" (1 Cor 16:17–18).

Gaius: a Christian from Macedonia who became a traveling companion of Paul, was with him in Ephesus (Acts 19:29, 20:4), hosted Paul and the church in Corinth (Rom 16:23), and was one of the few people that Paul personally baptized (1 Cor 1:14); probably not the same Gaius who was a leader of a Johannine church plant (3 John 1).

Hermogenes: Christian associated with Phygelus from Asia Minor who later abandoned Paul (2 Tim 1:15).

James: not the son of Zebedee (killed by Herod Agrippa recorded in Acts 12:2), but a brother of Jesus (Mark 6:3), who later became a prominent leader of the Christian community in Jerusalem (Acts 12:17; 15:13; 21:18; 1 Cor 15:7; Gal 1:19; 2:9; cf. James 1:1); Paul called him an apostle (Gal 1:19), although there were some tensions between Paul and some "people from James" who insisted that non-Jewish Christians must be circumcised (Gal 2:12).

Jason: a Jewish Christian who housed Paul and Silas in Thessalonica and was arrested because of his association with them (Acts 17:5–9); possibly, but probably not the same as the Jason mentioned in Romans 16:21 (see Lucius below).

Judas also called Barsabbas: not Judas Iscariot, nor the same as Joseph Barsabbas (below); an early disciple sent as a representative of the community in Jerusalem to the Christians in Antioch after the "Council of Jerusalem." He and Silas were "leaders among the brothers" (Acts 15:22) and messengers (15:27) and "prophets" (15:32).

Justus also called Jesus: one of only a few Jews ("ones of the circumcision") among Paul's coworkers; Paul conveys greetings from Justus to the Colossians, a comfort to him (Col 4:11).

Linus: Paul conveyed greetings to Timothy from Eubulus, Pudens, Linus, and Claudia (2 Tim 4:21).

Lois: the grandmother of Timothy (2 Tim 1:5).

Lucius: Paul conveyed to the Romans the greetings of "Lucius and Jason and Sosipater, my relatives" (Rom 16:21); he is probably a different person from the following two.

Lucius of Cyrene: one of the "prophets and teachers" of the church in Antioch, named along with Barnabas, Simeon called Niger, Manaean (a Herodian), and Saul (Acts 13:1).

Luke: described as "the beloved physician," sent greetings to the Colossians (Col 4:14) and Philemon (Phlm 24), was with Paul again later according to 2 Timothy 4:11.

Lydia: a female merchant ("seller of purple cloth") from Thyatira, a "worshiper of God" (possibly a Jewish proselyte) who was Paul's first convert in Philippi (Acts 16:11–15); Paul briefly stayed in her house after being released from prison (Acts 16:40).

Manaen (Acts 13:1).

Mark/John Mark: a young Christian from Jerusalem at whose mother's house Peter stayed (Acts 12:12), an early missionary associate of Paul and Barnabas (12:25; 13:5, 13; 15:37–39), called the "cousin" (nephew?) of Barnabas (Col 4:10), involved in preaching to the Christians in Colosse (Phlm 24); Paul later called him "useful in my ministry" (2 Tim 4:11).

Mnason: a Christian from Cyprus, who gave Paul and companions hospitality on their journey to Jerusalem (Acts 21:16).

Nympha: a Christian who hosted the community of believers in Colosse; Paul greeted her and "the church in her house" (Col 4:15).

Onesimus: a slave belonging to Philemon but converted to Christianity through Paul's ministry (who calls him "son" in Phlm 10); Paul asked Philemon to free Onesimus, so that he can become a "useful" brother (i.e., a missionary Phlm 11–15). He later evidently did become a Christian leader (Col 4:9).

Onesiphorus: a faithful benefactor; Paul sent greetings to his household in Ephesus (2 Tim 1:16; 4:19).

Philemon: a Colossian convert and coworker of Paul; Paul pleaded for him to release his slave Onesimus (Phlm 1).

Phoebe: deaconness of the church at Cenchreae (a port of Corinth) and benefactor of Paul, whom Paul recommends and who probably delivered Paul's letter to the Roman church (Rom 16:1–2).

Phygelus and Hermogenes: Christians in Asia Minor who later abandoned Paul (2 Tim 1:15).

Prisca: see Aquila for six references.

Pudens (2 Tim 4:21).

Quartus: Paul called him "our brother," and conveyed his greetings to the Christians in Rome (Rom 16:23).

Secundus: a Christian from Thessalonica who accompanied Paul on his final journey to Jerusalem (Acts 20:4).

Silvanus [Silas]: a Christian leader from Jerusalem who became Paul's key teammate after Barnabas separated from Paul; he worked with Paul and Timothy during their initial preaching in Macedonia and Achaia.

Simeon Niger (Acts 13:1).

Sopater, son of Pyrrhus: a Christian from Berea who accompanied Paul on his final journey to Jerusalem (Acts 20:4).

Sosipater: see Lucius.

Sosthenes: an official of the Jewish synagogue at Corinth who became a Christian; Paul called him a "brother" (1 Cor 1:1; Acts 18:17).

Stephanas: a Christian from Corinth, Paul's first convert in Achaia (1 Cor 1:16; 16:15–18).

Syntyche (Phil 4:2–3).

Tertius: Paul's secretary who sent his own greetings to the Christians in Rome (Rom 16:22).

Timothy: Paul's closest missionary companion.

Titius Justus: a "worshiper of God" (Jewish proselyte) in whose house Paul stayed and preached in Corinth (Acts 18:7).

Titus: a missionary who worked very closely with Paul as one of his closest companions.

Trophimus: a Christian from Ephesus in Asia who traveled with Paul for a while (Acts 20:4; 21:29); Paul left him ill in Miletus (2 Tim 4:20).

Tychicus: another traveling companion of Paul from Asia (Acts 20:4), Paul's messenger to the Ephesians, Colossians, and Titus, delivering news and encouragement (Eph 6:21–22, Col 4:7–9, 2 Tim 4:12, Titus 3:12).

Zenas: a lawyer whom Paul told Titus to send along with Apollos, seeing "that they lack nothing" (Titus 3:13).

The following people are mentioned in the list of people to whom Paul sends greetings in Romans 16:3–16.

Ampliatus: Paul greets him as "my beloved in the Lord" (Rom 16:8).

Andronicus and Junia: a husband/wife team, or possibly a brother/sister pair of missionaries, whom Paul calls "my relatives" and "prominent among the apostles;" they were in prison with him at some point and were Christians even before Paul was (Rom 16:7).

Apelles: Paul greets him as "approved in Christ" (Rom 16:10).

Aristobulus: Paul greets the members of his family (Rom 16:10).

Asyncritus: Paul greets "Asyncritus, Phlegon, Hermes, Patrobas, Hermas, and the brothers with them," but we know nothing else about any of these early Christians (Rom 16:14).

Epaenetus: Paul greets him as "my beloved" and "the first fruits (i.e., first convert) in Asia" (Rom 16:5).

Hermas (Rom 16:14).

Hermes (Rom 16:14).

Herodion: Paul greets him as "my relative" (Rom 16:11).

Julia (Rom 16:15).

Junia (Rom 16:7).

Mary: Paul greets her, telling the Christians in Rome "she has worked very hard among you" (Rom 16:6).

Narcissus: Paul greets the members of his family who are "in the Lord" (Rom 16:11).

Nereus and his sister (Rom 16:15).

Olympas (Rom 16:15).

Patrobas (Rom 16:14).

Persis: Paul greets him as "the beloved," saying "he has worked hard in the Lord" (Rom 16:12).

Philologus: Paul greets "Philologus, Julia, Nereus and his sister, and Olympas, and all the saints who are with them." They are probably members of a house-church in Rome, but we know nothing else about them (Rom 16:15).

Phlegon (Rom 16:14).

Rufus and his mother: Paul greets them, calling Rufus "chosen in the Lord," and describing his mother as "a mother to me also" (Rom 16:13).

Stachys: Paul greets him as "my beloved" (Rom 16:9).

Tryphaena: Paul greets them (and Tryphosa) as "workers in the Lord" (Rom 16:12).

Tryphosa: Paul greets them (and Tryphaena) as "workers in the Lord" (Rom 16:12).

Urbanus: Paul greets him as a " fellow worker in Christ" (Rom 16:9).

That's an amazing list of coworkers and teammates that Paul mentions by name! And no doubt many more people were members of Paul's extended ministry team who aren't listed in the New Testament. That's a staggering thought.

Conclusion

The accomplishment of ministry is never achieved alone. Ministry is all about collaboration, cooperation, networking, interdependence, sharing and teamwork and working together. Ministry involves training other people, who will in turn train others to train even more people.

When you investigate the New Testament coworkers of Paul, you see just how important it is to be solidly connected in a cooperative effort as you serve the Lord. How would you rate the value you place on teambuilding and collaboration?

PERSPECTIVES ON THE HEART OF A SHEPHERD

5

Motivation for Ministry

WHY DO I SERVE in ministry? What foundational motives lie behind what I do? These are important questions for pastors to ask themselves, yet answering them may be more complicated than it seems at first.

It's Complicated

Evaluating our motives in ministry is never easy. The apostle Paul admitted as much in 1 Corinthians 4:3–4. There he wrote that he cared little about the evaluative judgment of the Corinthians or even his self-evaluation and judgment. He was solely concerned with the appraisal and estimation of the Lord, which wouldn't be revealed "until the Lord comes who will both bring to life the hidden things of darkness and reveal the counsels [i.e., motives] of the hearts" (v. 5). Remember humans are usually satisfied with whatever *looks* good. God probes for what *is* good. And the motive-judging day won't come until the end of our lives here on earth, and then the Lord will reveal the secrets of each minister's heart.

This matter is further complicated by the fact that our hearts can deceive us, crying out with selfish desires, and we can misinterpret the motives that lie behind our actions. Proverbs 21:2 says, "every way of a man is right in his own eyes." We justify ourselves and excuse our sinful behavior or attitudes, all the while posturing for position and seeking the fulfillment of our agendas. Thinking the best of ourselves, we dangerously underestimate our propensity to sinful and selfish ambitions. We would do well to remember the truth of Jeremiah 17:9 when evaluating ourselves: "The heart is deceitful above all things, and desperately wicked (NKJV)."

Evaluating ministry motives is also complicated by another profound reality: we cannot see inside the hearts and minds of others. We're unable to judge the reasons people do what they do, yet we see this attempted by many Christians who suspiciously attribute incorrect motives behind the actions of other brothers, forgetting completely that we can't fully understand the mystery of their motives.

So before evaluating ministry motives, we need to remember three things. It is the Lord who will perfectly judge motives. We can't always evaluate our motives correctly. And we'll never be able to assess the reasons other people make the ministry choices they do.

We need to examine the Scriptures and see what should motivate us as God's people to minister in our pagan society. Evaluating (or trying to evaluate) ministry motives is essential. And perhaps it would be easier to begin evaluating ministry motives by looking at what should not be motivating factors.

What Should Not Motivate Us

No pastor or any other Christian worker should be motivated by self-interests, as though the work of the ministry is all about you and what will benefit you most. This to me is so obvious, yet all too often the top priority for some Christian leaders seems to be the question "what's in it for me?" What's best for you should not be your ultimate concern; what honors Christ and what glorifies him should be.

Nor should you be motivated by a desire for power and control. Decades ago, one writer described a self-absorbed Christian leader he knew as "a kind of one-man army of the Lord. He is commander in chief, master sergeant, corporal, and private. He is the bride at every wedding and the corpse at every funeral."[53] Tragically, that man believed everything in ministry revolved around him.

This kind of assessment can never be made of a true servant of Christ! Achieving and then keeping one's positions of power was foreign for first-century Christians to conceive. They saw themselves as "strangers and aliens" in their world and "citizens of heaven" who ministered in this life for the glory of their King. Many were put to death for this very worldview. They didn't die so they could gain power, or retain influence, or control their world. They were killed for exactly the opposite—their unwillingness to enter into the sinful idolatry and activities of a pagan culture.

We shouldn't try to minister to be relevant, as though cultural relevance were our goal. In fact, the gospel will confront a culture and challenge its

---

53 Weldon Grassland, *Better Leader for Your Church* (New York: Abingdon, 1955), 14.

foundations. A generation ago, G. Campbell Morgan wrote, "the spirit of the city of Corinth had entered the church.... Our work is not to catch the spirit of the age; it is to correct it."[54] Those today who want to be culturally relevant in ministry had better be careful they are confronting and correcting American culture more than uncritically and unbiblically reflecting it.

We shouldn't minister because we're motivated by anger. Sin is ugly and should cause a righteous reaction of indignation. But the anger often displayed by "Christian activists" hardly seems righteous (such as hateful groups like one church with its "God hates fags" signs). In contrast, the angry riot in Acts 19 at Ephesus is a great illustration of reaching unbelievers. The Christians in Ephesus preached the gospel, not politics, and were known as "followers of the Way" (vv. 9, 23). They were NOT known as "anti-Artemis people" or "picketers of the Temple" or "Idolaters Anonymous." They were passionate about the beautiful Christ, not angry against the ugly Artemis.

We shouldn't try to minister in our increasingly pagan culture to gain favor and be well-liked by unbelievers. Certainly, we don't want to push them away with an offensive personality (for that wouldn't be Christ-like). But to construct a philosophy of ministry ultimately designed to win approval from unbelievers is not Scriptural. Our Lord said, "I always do the things that are pleasing to him [the Father]" in John 8:29. The approval of an unbeliever didn't control our Savior's motivation, nor should it control ours.

Popularity, fame, and affirmation by the world can be perilous for the man of God. Over three hundred fifty years ago Thomas Brooks wrote that Satan presents "the world in its beauty so as to bewitch us ... and eventually to destroy. Where one thousand are destroyed by the world's frowns, ten thousand are destroyed by the world's smiles."[55]

So we return to the questions—"Why do I serve in ministry? What foundational motives lie behind what I do?" It can't be to retain power, or to be relevant, or because we're angry, or because we want approval from unbelievers.

What Should Motivate Us

The time when I defined who I was in ministry was in my first full-time pastorate immediately following seminary. I was a pastor in Utah with a mis-

---

54 G. Campbell Morgan, *The Corinthian Letters of Paul* (Old Tappan, NJ: Fleming H. Revell, 1956), 27.

55 Thomas Brooks, *Precious Remedies against Satan's Devices* (Edinburgh, Scotland: Banner of Truth Trust, 1968), 102.

sion church of twelve people surrounded by a city of almost 150,000. I was obscure and insignificant and in the wilderness. That is where God worked mightily on what motivated me in ministry.

Where you are unknown and unnoticed, serving quietly in a hidden place, your ministry motives become sharpened. Only God knows what you are doing, and you learn to rest in him and his approval. In Utah, I quietly served him, waiting for growth in the ministry until he brought it. And that was a long, painful wait.

In Utah, I learned that preaching and teaching to a group was the way to appeal to many, but the quiet work of equipping a few was more influential and lasting. It wasn't more exciting, but it was more productive. Richard Baxter wrote,

> I have found by experience, that some ignorant persons, who have been so long unprofitable hearers, have got more knowledge and remorse of conscience in half an hour's close discourse, than they did from ten years' public preaching. I know that preaching the gospel publicly is the most excellent means, because we speak to many at once. But it is usually far more effectual to preach it privately to a particular sinner.[56]

I also learned in Utah the spiritual benefit of personal obscurity as opposed to personal advancement. Jeremiah cautioned, "And do you seek great things for yourself? Seek them not" (Jer 45:5). Personal ambition is such a shallow, empty motivation. Yet it captivates all too many men in ministry whose drive for fame consumes them (yes, pastors can think that way).

We should think another way. We should think like Jesus, who always did everything to please the Father. We must reach this increasingly pagan society because God, in his providence, placed us here at this time, to reflect his love and holiness to the unbelievers of our day. He is the one we serve, and he is the one who will judge our motives. So we'd better seek to please him and not the unbelievers of our world or the people of our church. The formula for success is to seek always to please the Father. The formula for failure is to try to please everybody, or anybody else.

We close with two vital passages that must inform our motivation for ministry:

---

56 Richard Baxter, *The Reformed Pastor* (Edinburgh, Scotland: Banner of Truth Trust, 2007), 18.

Bondservants, obey in everything those who are your earthly masters, not by way of eyeservice, as people-pleasers, but with sincerity of heart, fearing the Lord. Whatever you do, work heartily, as for the Lord and not for men, knowing that from the Lord you will receive the inheritance as your reward. You are serving the Lord Christ (Col 3:22–24).

But just as we have been approved by God to be entrusted with the gospel, so we speak, not as to please men, but to please God who tests our hearts (1 Thess 2:4).

6

Humility, Brokenness, and Ministry

ONE OF THE MOST important values in today's American culture is fame. Guys want to play in an NCAA football championship or a Final Four basketball championship or in the NFL or NBA, and become famous. Everyone seems to want to do something that blows up social media, and they admire the person with an incredible number of followers on their social media feed. One girl put it this way: "Becoming famous is the chief goal of my life."

We've become fixated on fame, worshipping at the altar of celebrity as fame junkies. And tragically, people in ministry can become just as obsessed with fame. An unattributed quote often linked to Count Zinzendorf offers a compelling challenge: "Preach the gospel, die, and be forgotten." It's a stirring call—but a difficult path to walk.

Back in the early 20th century, one pastor walked that hard road in Quebec. D. A. Carson wrote about his dad in a biography honoring his father, who was a pastor who served humbly and in obscurity in Canada:

> Most of us, however, serve in modest patches. Most pastors will not regularly preach to thousands, let alone tens of thousands. They will not write influential books, they will not supervise large staffs, and they will never see more than modest growth. They will plug away at their care for the aged, at their visitation, at their counseling, at their Bible studies and preaching. Some will work with so little support that they will prepare their own bulletins. They cannot possibly discern whether the constraints of their own sphere of service owe more to the specific challenges of the local situation or to their own shortcomings. Once in a while they will cast a wistful eye on "successful" ministries. Many of them will attend the conferences sponsored by the revered masters and come away with a

slightly discordant combination of, on the one hand, gratitude and encouragement and, on the other, jealousy, feelings of inadequacy, and guilt. Most of us—let us be frank—are ordinary pastors . . . let the voice and ministry of the ordinary pastor be heard, for such servants have much to teach us.[57]

The walk of humility, brokenness, and obscurity is a difficult one for pastors. Where does it begin?

God's Glory Crushes Pride, Brings Humility

In Deuteronomy 8, Moses warned the people to remain humble, using the Hebrew word *anah*, which means "to bow down" in Deuteronomy 8: 2, 3, 16. In Deuteronomy 8:14, Moses warned the people against having a proud heart, using the Hebrew word *rûm* which is elsewhere used about an upraised formation of rocks. The imagery is vivid—a proud heart is uplifted and hard. Moses repeated the same warning in Deuteronomy 17:20 with the same Hebrew word *rûm*, only that warning was directed to the future kings of Israel. They were not to have prideful, uplifted hearts of stone.

Another powerful Hebrew word describes the opposite of a proud, uplifted heart of stone—*dakah*, which is also used regarding crushed, pulverized rocks. This word is used in Psalm 34:18 ("the LORD . . . saves the crushed in spirit") and describes the opposite of the hardened, proud hearts of stone. God is near the one who has been crushed and is humble. This Hebrew word is often translated as "contrite" and is used once in Psalm 51:17b (". . . a contrite heart, O God, you will not despise") and twice in Isaiah 57:15 ("For thus says the One who is high and lifted up, . . . 'I dwell in the high and holy place, and also with him who is of a contrite and lowly spirit, to revive the spirit of the lowly, and to revive the heart of the contrite'").

In the Old Testament, the Hebrew word for "glory" is *kabod*, and it means "to be heavy, weighty." This word describes God's glory—his person is substantive, while we as humans are all lightness and nothingness in comparison. Under God's *kabod*, under his glory, we are crushed and broken.

Men in the Bible Who Were Crushed

God's glory is crushing. Our pathetic, weak, worthless, feeble, puny pride gets crushed under the heavy weightiness of God's awesome glory and holi-

---

[57] D. A. Carson, *Memoirs of an Ordinary Pastor: The Life and Reflections of Tom Carson* (Wheaton, IL: Crossway, 2008), 9.

ness. There are a number of examples of men in the Bible who were crushed by the glory of God.

> **Job**—after debating with his friends over the reasons and meaning of his trials, heard from God in his majesty. Here's his response to God's revelation of his glory: "I despise myself and repent in dust and ashes" (Job 42:6).
>
> **Moses**—after forty years of quietness as a shepherd, encountered God's glory at the burning bush, and it says: "Moses trembled and did not dare to look" (Acts 7:32).
>
> **Isaiah**—the godly court prophet, who had been faithfully serving the Lord, saw the LORD high and lifted up in his glory and responded this way: "woe is me! I am undone [lit. destroyed]" (Isaiah 6:5).
>
> **Ezekiel**—after seeing the vision of God in his throne room "fell on his face" (Ezekiel 1:28).
>
> **Nebuchadnezzar**—after his incredible pride was crushed with a seven-year bout of insanity, spoke these incredible words: "At the end of the days I, Nebuchadnezzar, lifted my eyes to heaven, and my reason returned to me, and I blessed the Most High, and praised and honored him who lives forever, for his dominion is an everlasting dominion, and his kingdom endures from generation to generation; all the inhabitants of the earth are accounted as nothing, and he does according to his will among the host of heaven and among the inhabitants of the earth; and none can stay his hand or say to him, 'What have you done?'" (Daniel 4:34–35).
>
> **Peter**—after fishing all night, obeyed the Lord with reluctance and caught a huge load of fish. Then Peter realized how proud and arrogant he was and responded, "Depart from me, for I am a sinful man, O Lord" (Luke 5:8).
>
> **John**—the closest of Jesus' earthly companions, saw the Risen Lord Jesus in his glory on the Isle of Patmos, and Revelation records that "When I saw him, I fell at his feet as though dead" (Rev 1:17).

As these men in the Bible, our pride should get crushed under the heavy weightiness of God's awesome glory and holiness. This crushing should lead us to greater usefulness in ministry, but sadly, this is not always the case.

Some Demonstrations of Pride

Here are some subtle (and not so subtle) demonstrations of pride in the lives of many pastors and other Christian leaders I've observed. I'm ashamed to say, I've been guilty of many of these in my own life.

- Prayerlessness and relying on your own abilities, strength, and self-sufficiency.
- Unwillingness to listen to advice, instruction, correction, information, and/or suggestions.
- Reluctance to submit to authority, even anyone else's set of rules.
- Arguing and quarreling to prove you're always right, even to the point of anger and rage.
- Dominating conversations, saying something about every subject on every occasion ("with my vast store of wisdom, it seems a pity not to tell others how to handle all their questions and difficulties").
- Maintaining an unteachable spirit (because you already know everything you need to know).
- Responding to everyone around you with mockery, ridicule, and sarcastic put-downs, yet you are unable to laugh at yourself along with everyone else.
- Eagerly promoting yourself, who you know, what you've done, magnifying your achievements, illustrating your conversations with all the times you were right or you came to the rescue.
- Enjoying the admiration of others, even secretly reveling in it.
- Unwillingness to submit to the small indignities of daily life (standing in a line, waiting your turn, driving an older used car, performing menial tasks, or doing some manual labor).
- An over-concern with externals, appearances, numbers (all designed to make you look good).
- A reluctance to associate with people who can't advance your status or enhance your image (the poor, the shut-ins/infirmed, the severely handicapped, the elderly, or children).
- Always wanting to be in the role of the teacher and an unwillingness to listen to others as a student.

- Being unwilling to admit you are wrong, apologize, or seek forgiveness.
- Controlling meetings by commenting on every subject and demanding your solution(s) be the final outcome for every agenda item.
- Ungrateful for your present circumstances ("I deserve better . . . larger . . . more significant").
- Constantly having your family in charge, or up front, or in the spotlight.
- Correcting others, even if they don't ask for it ("they so desperately need my advice").
- Sinful pride in you and/or your family's intellectual development, acquisition of knowledge, academic achievement, class rankings, prestigious scholarships, awards/honors/trophies.
- Knowing the truth, and defending the truth, because you are right (and you are!) . . . but doing so from a position of spiritual superiority and pride because it feels so good to be right.
- Deep discontentment that you're not more famous, better known, in a bigger ministry, with tens of thousands of people downloading your sermons each week.

Conclusion

If we fail to renounce our pride and submit to the glory of the awesome King of the Universe, then we will experience the tragedy stated in 1 Peter 5:5. "Clothe yourselves, all of you, with humility toward one another, for 'God opposes the proud but gives grace to the humble.'"

God can use us only if we are humble and broken. If we fail to clothe ourselves with humility, God will oppose us. The Bible doesn't say he will passively remove his blessing from us. It says he will **actively oppose** us. Can you imagine anything worse than being actively opposed by the Lord God Almighty, all the while deceiving yourself into thinking you're serving him?

May God help us to see his glory and respond with humility, by renouncing all of our pride. And may we leave the matter of our place and reputation in ministry to God as we preach the gospel, die, and then are forgotten.

7

Passion for Ministry

THERE IS AN AMAZING exuberance in the early days of ministry. God's call is so fresh, his will so clear, his work so exhilarating.

But over time, I've observed that many pastors and Christian leaders reach a point where they feel they've given the ministry all they've got. They become lethargic, even lazy. They coast on past glories, lose focus, and become cynical. Their commitment wanes. Hobbies become dominant rather than providing a mere distraction. Then, after further reflection, they decide to give up. And as they shut down, they are left wondering—what happened to the passion? What happened to the unquenchable fire, the burning drive, the fire of conviction? Where did my passion for ministry go?

There are numerous reasons for a loss of passion for ministry. The list of things which can reduce or take away passion is virtually endless. However, the real reason for the loss of passion is not found in the externalities of ministry. Passion is an internal issue. It is a spiritual issue which is intimately related to the strength of your relationship to Jesus Christ.

A Wrong Passion

Passion based on and driven by externals is a worldly passion. It is subject to change, erosion, and destruction. This type of passion takes us on an emotional roller coaster ride. It makes us feel happy and excited going up, and then sad and unfulfilled on the way down. One major cause for the loss of passion in the ministry is that we become passionate for the wrong things. In fact, passion for things is a misguided, idolatrous passion.

Godly passion is founded on, and is a natural extension of, those things which are the essentials of faith. Christ-honoring passion is constantly energized by a deep and sincere spirituality, rooted in grace alone, and is the result of the indwelling Holy Spirit's power. This passion can't be manufactured. It's not merely the cause of our ministry efforts, but it is the resultant overflow of our personal, growing relationship with Christ.

Leadership literature, secular and Christian, often speaks of having a passion for the organization, for the task, for the results, or for the vision. Sadly, this overlooks the most important aspect of passion. A godly passion is always relational. It is relationship-based. There is no godly passion without relationship, and there can be no passion for ministry without a growing relationship with Jesus Christ.

The Passion of Paul

You can certainly feel the passion Paul had for Christ and for the ministry as you read the New Testament. To cite just one example, go to the epistle to the Philippians.

In Philippians 3:7–10, Paul described his passion for Christ above everything else: "I count all things but loss for the excellency of the knowledge of Christ Jesus my Lord, for whom I have suffered the loss of all things, and do count them but dung . . . that I may know him, and the power of his resurrection, and the fellowship of his sufferings" (vv. 8, 10). Everything considered a loss, everything considered dung compared to the knowledge of Christ—strong words expressing the fire of godly passion.

Earlier in the letter, in Philippians 2:17, Paul wrote that he was being "poured out as a drink offering." That is such an obscure analogy to modern ears, but when properly understood, it is so powerful. It deserves a full explanation.

The Drink Offering

The Old Testament sacrifice called the drink offering is one of the earliest recorded offerings/sacrifices found in the Bible. It is one of only two known to have been offered before the giving of the Law (the other being the burnt offering). We read of Jacob offering the drink offering five hundred years before Moses in Genesis 35:14: "And Jacob set up a pillar in the place where he had spoken with him, a pillar of stone. He poured out a drink offering on it, and he poured oil on it."

According to the Law of Moses, the drink offering consisted of wine (Num 15:5) poured around the altar (Exod 30:9). It was joined with burnt offerings (Num 6:15,17) and could be presented daily (Exod 29:40), on the Sabbath (Num 28:9), or on feast days (Num 28:14).

The drink offerings were to be composed of "strong wine" (Num 28:7). This corresponds to the animal sacrifices which had to be without blemish in all respects (Lev 22:17–25) and the meal offering which was composed of fine flour with the exclusion of leaven and honey (Lev 2:11). The wine was to be pure, in the sense that it was not to be watered down.

The amount of wine was also regulated. One-fourth of a hin of wine was required if the burnt offering were one lamb (one hin is equivalent to one gallon), one-third of a hin/gallon for a ram, and one-half of a hin/gallon for a bull (Num15:5; 28:7,14).

Both the Jewish and the pagan world understood the sacrifice of the drink offering. The process went like this. The one making the drink offering came and stood before the altar after the animal was killed and while it burned on the altar. At some point during the burning, the drink offering was poured out as the final sacrificial act. They poured out the wine either on the ground in front of the altar or on top of the burning sacrifice (in which case it would vaporize immediately into steam and go into the air). The steam would symbolize the rising of that sacrifice into the nostrils of the deity for whom it was being offered. The Old Testament drink offering would rise up to the LORD, demonstrating supreme willingness to sacrifice oneself for God's glory.

In Philippians 2:17, Paul used the present passive tense of the verb indicating that he was being poured out continually like a burnt offering. He saw his entire life as a sacrifice offered to Christ. How many of us can honestly say we are exhilarated with joy in the sacrifices we make for the cause of Christ?

F.B. Meyer has written these words regarding this kind of passion in ministry:

> It is certain that before any service we do for God or man is to be of lasting or permanent benefit, it must be saturated with our heart's blood. That which costs us nothing will not benefit others. If there is no expenditure of tears and prayer . . . it will profit nothing. Let us rather seek to be poured forth as an offering than to do much without feeling the least travail of soul. As the fertility of Egypt in any year is in direct proportion to the height that the waters of the Nile measure, so the amount of our real fruitfulness in the world is gauged by the expenditure of our spiritual force. It was because Moses was prepared to be blotted from the book of God for his people that he carried them for forty years through the desert and deposited them on the very borders of the Promised

Land. It was because Jesus wept over Jerusalem that He was able to send a Pentecost on that guilty city. It was because Paul was prepared to be accursed for his brethren according to the flesh that he was able to turn so many from darkness to light and from the power of Satan unto God. No heart pangs, no spiritual seed.[58]

Two Other Men of Passion

In Philippians 2:17–30, Paul wrote about the passion he and Timothy and Epaphroditus had for their ministry to the Philippians. These other two men also shared Paul's passion.

Timothy's focus was on the Lord. Paul states that, unlike many others, Timothy was not seeking after his own interests but those of Jesus Christ (2:21). Timothy served with Paul in the furtherance of the gospel (2:22). Christ and the gospel were at the passionate center of Timothy's life.

Epaphroditus was also a faithful servant whose focus was on the things of Christ. He had pushed himself almost to the point of death to bring the gift to Paul from the Philippian church. Maybe he grew ill on the six-week journey and pushed himself beyond his limits to get to the apostle's side. Or, perhaps after arriving, he contracted some illness but kept pushing himself in his service to Paul in the cause of the gospel. His longing and concern for the church back in Philippi reveal his passion for the things of Christ.

Paul called Epaphroditus a "minister to my need" (2:25) and stated that Epaphroditus had completed by his presence what the Philippians could not do in their absence in "service" to Paul (2:30).

The word translated "minister" and "service" comes from a Greek word from which we get our word "liturgy." In secular Greek, the word was used of a man who, out of love for his city and his gods, would finance a great drama or outfit a battleship. This word has the flavor of sacred service or worship. Every servant of Jesus Christ does what he does, whether giving or helping or speaking, as a passionate offering to the Lord Jesus. His heart is centered on the Lord Jesus Christ and his work.

Paul mentioned that Epaphroditus risked his life (2:30). The Greek word is a picturesque one which signifies hazarding, risking, or throwing the dice in gambling. Epaphroditus literally gambled with his life. He rolled the dice on his life and became sick near to death for the sake of fulfilling

---

58 F. B. Meyer, *Devotional Commentary on Philippians* (Grand Rapids: Kregel), 111–112.

his ministry. That's passion! The work of the gospel involves both physical and emotional hardships that can wear us down, but the passion of knowing Christ and growing in that knowledge is able to keep the devotion for ministry hot.

Attitudes Accompanying Passion

Three attitudes will mark those servants whose passion is focused on the Lord Jesus Christ. These attitudes are as follows.

They are willing to be sent anywhere.

It wouldn't have been easy for Timothy to leave the side of Paul, his beloved father in the faith, to go to Philippi. But he was willing to go if that was God's will. It wasn't easy for Epaphroditus to leave the comforts of home in Philippi and journey to Rome, but he did it. Then it would be difficult for Epaphroditus to leave Paul and return home, but he was willing to go where the Lord wanted him. Passionate people are willing to go anywhere.

They are willing to serve anyone.

Timothy served Paul, but he was willing to go and serve the Philippian church. Epaphroditus served the Philippian church, but he was willing to go and serve Paul. A servant with a passion for Christ isn't out to make a name for himself by speaking to large crowds only. He's available to his Lord to serve anyone the Lord directs him to serve.

They are willing to sacrifice anything.

Timothy had given up his own interests to become a servant of Christ. Epaphroditus almost lost his life in his service for the Lord. To the Ephesian elders, Paul said this about his own ministry, "But I do not account my life of any value nor as precious to myself, if only I may finish my course and the ministry that I received from the Lord Jesus, to testify to the gospel of the grace of God" (Acts 20:24). People with passion are willing to sacrifice anything and everything.

Sadly, many who serve the Lord, including some in full-time ministry, do it with mixed motives. They're out for the acclaim others can give them. They like being in the limelight. They manipulate and use people for their own advancement or gain. They need the job. Those types of servants will lose their passion. Their fire for ministry will become extinguished, and ultimately, they will be relegated to the sidelines.

Serving Christ isn't easy. The term "fellow soldier" (Phil 2:25) implies warfare, and this brings us under the withering attacks of the enemy, who wants to hinder the cause of Christ. Paul was in prison due to persecution from without, but he was also under attack from those who preached the gospel from envy and selfish ambition (Phil 1:15, 17). Perhaps they are the ones he refers to in Philippians 2:21. They claimed to be serving Christ, but in reality they were serving themselves. Over 100 years ago, Alexander Maclaren wrote: "Many a professing Christian life has a veneer of godliness nailed thinly over a solid bulk of selfishness."[59] Paul knew the keen disappointment of professing Christians who were not faithful because they were living for themselves.

Paul was a passionate man whose chief end in life was to know Christ and serve him faithfully until his death. Timothy was a passionate man who was consumed not with his own interest but with the interest of Christ. Epaphroditus was a passionate man who gambled with his life for the cause of Christ.

Passionate people look at trials and difficulties, hard places, physical discomfort, pain, and even death as the cost of serving their glorious Savior. When you get to the point where you passionately, even recklessly, abandon yourself to the will of God to be pleasing in his sight, nothing is dark, nothing is forbidding, light is shed on everything, and ultimate sacrifice leads to ultimate joy. But if you have lost that kind of joy, ultimately it is because you've wandered in your relationship with your Lord. You've lost your passion for Jesus Christ.

The exuberance of the early days of ministry can return. God's call can once again be fresh. His work can again be exhilarating. But only if you repent of your shallow spirituality and return to your passion to know Christ and to grow in that knowledge.

---

59 Alexander Maclaren, "Philippians," *Expositions of Holy Scripture* (Grand Rapids: Baker Books, 1982 reprint), 284.

8

Jealousy and Envy

JEALOUSY, ENVY, RIVALRY. UGLY is not too strong a word to describe these sins. We read those words and recognize their sinful qualities. We know they're wrong. But it seems most of us can easily dismiss them as something fairly minor, as if no more than dandruff of the soul that we can simply brush off.

The more I've examined my own heart as a pastor, the more I've cringed at the ugliness of jealousy and the more I see its ugly tentacles wrapped around my heart and mind. It's not something insignificant. Jealousy is a sin that can entangle and corrupt my soul like an invisible barbed-wire. And if I do not repent of this sin, it can lead to bitter and vile emotions and actions like greed, covetousness, rivalry, hate, and murder.

The Bible's Catalog of Sins

The catalog of sins mentioned in the Bible is difficult to read and seriously consider. Throughout the first five books of the Bible all sorts of sins were forbidden and practiced and punished. The same is true in a most sweeping way throughout the Old Testament. Specifically in Proverbs 6:16–19 we read, "There are six things that the LORD hates, seven are an abomination to him: haughty eyes, a lying tongue, hands that shed innocent blood, a heart that devises wicked plans, feet that make haste to run to evil, a false witness who breathes out lies, and one who sows discord among brethren."

In the New Testament we read Galatians 5:19–21 and shudder: "Now the works of the flesh are evident: sexual immorality, impurity, sensuality, idolatry, sorcery, enmity, strife, jealousy, fits of anger, rivalries, dissensions, divisions, envy, drunkenness, orgies, and things like these" (Gal 5:19–21).

Just stop and see buried within that vile catalog of fifteen sins listed above, the supposedly minor and insignificant sins of jealousy and envy. That should give pause to the notion that these are mere dandruff of the soul.

What's striking to me is the fact that in the biblical catalog of sin, we find the sins of envy and jealousy. These sins are seen as profoundly significant in God's estimation, yet jealousy barely merits more than a casual brush-off in the hearts and minds of all too many pastors today.

Examples of Jealousy

What are some of the sad examples of jealousy? Pastors can become jealous of another pastor's:

- larger church and greater ministry recognition
- possessions, wealth, financial assets (this is what covetousness is)
- privileges, advantages, status
- looks, appearance, health
- personality, abilities, talents, skills
- awards, accomplishments, achievements, popularity
- intelligence, knowledge, education
- spouse, family, friends, relationships

Those are just a few examples. All of them could be summarized with these words by Jerry Bridges in his book *Respectable Sins*: "Envy is the painful and sometimes resentful awareness of an advantage enjoyed by someone else."[60] Such tragic words we can understand all too well.

Why Is Jealousy So Bad?

Now perhaps you are in agreement that envy and jealousy are bad ways for us to respond. But you may still be unconvinced. Are they really that bad? Aren't they more private sins that fail to rise to the level of even worse attitudes, actions, and responses? Can't they be brushed off since we are the only ones affected, and no one can see into our hearts?

Jealousy and envy are declared to be sin in the Scriptures. That is reason enough to seriously consider the sinfulness of these related sins. God declares these attitudes of the heart to be sinful.

---

60 Jerry Bridges, *Respectable Sins* (Colorado Springs: NavPress, 2007), 149.

However, God also says that such attitudes are demonic. In James 3:14–16 "But if you have bitter envy and self-seeking in your hearts, do not boast and lie against the truth. This wisdom does not descend from above, but is earthly, sensual, demonic. For where envy and self-seeking exist, confusion and every evil thing are there." When our heart devises its petty jealousies, we're thinking and acting like a demon!

A third reason envy and jealousy are so bad is because they lead to other depravities. When you allow such vile attitudes to fester, other sins are given a foothold into your soul. That's exactly what James 3:16 says, "For where jealousy and selfish ambition exist, there will be disorder and every vile practice." Jealousy leads to bitterness, which leads to hate, which leads to rivalries, which leads to violence, which leads to murder. That's what James 3:16 is implying. And that's what James 4:1–2 clearly states: "What causes quarrels and what causes fights among you? Is it not this, that your passions are at war within you? You desire and do not have, so you murder. You covet and cannot obtain, so you fight and quarrel." Not a beautiful portrayal of humanity. Jealousy is the murderous spirit of envious hate.

Defining the Words

It is helpful to understand the meaning of the words used in the Bible for the ugly attitudes being examined in this chapter. Similar words are used in both Testaments of the Bible.

In the Old Testament, the Hebrew word used is *qana*, meaning "zealous" or "jealous" depending on the context. In Genesis 37:11 Joseph's brothers were "jealous of him," and their jealousy led them to fake his death and sell him into slavery in Egypt. A similar use of *qana* in the negative is found in Numbers 5:14, 20 referring to a husband who is jealous of his wife's behavior.

But *qana* is also used in contexts where zeal and acts of deep devotion are seen in a positive light. Phineas was commended by the Lord for being "zealous for God" (Num 25:11,13 NKJV). Elijah claimed he was "very zealous for the LORD God" (1 Kgs 19:10, 14 NKJV).

And then the word *qana* is used in a number of passages referring to God's jealousy for his people, a holy jealousy based on his claim for an exclusive relationship (Deut 4:24, 5:9, 6:15; Josh 24:19; Ezek 39:25; Nah 1:2). In fact, the reason God gives for the second commandment is "I, the LORD your God, am a jealous God" (Exod 20:5). Because they followed pagan gods, God was jealous of Israel (Deut 32:16, 21; Zech 1:14, 8:2).

In the New Testament, two Greek words are used to describe jealousy and envy, both of which are found in Galatians 5:20–21. The word translated "jealousy" is the Greek word *zēlos*, from which we get the English "zeal," literally meaning "heat" or "come to boil."[61] Figuratively, it's used in two ways (like *qana* in the Old Testament): positively, it's a great enthusiasm for a cause, a person, or an object, which we normally refer to as zeal; negatively, it's the darker side of envy or jealousy. In the New Testament *zēlos* is thus translated either as "zeal" or "godly jealousy" (John 2:17, Rom 10:2, 1 Cor 12:31, 2 Cor 7:11) or as "envy" or "jealousy" (Acts 5:17, Rom 13:13, 1 Cor 13:4, Jas 3:14,16).

A useful summary of all the above is given once again by Jerry Bridges: "There are legitimate occasions for jealousy, such as when someone is trying to win your spouse away from you.... Sinful jealousy occurs, however, when we are afraid someone is going to become equal to or even superior to us."[62] The root emotion of jealousy is pride, which leads to the fear that someone, somewhere has an advantage over us and will overtake our place in life.

The second Greek word used in the New Testament is the word *phthonos*. Unlike *zēlos*, this second word is used positively only once (Jas 4:5 referring to God's Spirit jealously yearning for us). The word *phthonos* is translated most often by the word "envy." Pilate knew the Jews handed Jesus over to him for trial out of envy (Mark 15:10). In Galatians 5:21, *phthonos* is listed in that catalog of sins and translated envy, and then the verb form in 5:26 is translated as "envying." In Titus 3:3 it's used as a description of our past lives outside of Christ: "For we ourselves were once foolish, disobedient, led astray, slaves to various passions and pleasures, passing our days in malice and *phthonos*, hated by others and hating one another." The idea behind the word is a sense of rivalry due to ill-will and spite.

Together jealousy and envy germinate in the soil of pride. They lead to an unhealthy competitiveness that demands and aggressively seeks to be number one in every circumstance.

Rivalry is another way of describing this twisted attitude, which always needs to be the center of attention, always on top, always in charge, always the best. It can never take the back seat, nor will it ever leave center stage. Not being recognized and not being in control are things to be avoided at all cost.

---

61 Bauer, Arndt and Gingrich, *A Greek-English Lexicon of the New Testament and Other Early Christian Literature*, 2nd ed. (Chicago: University of Chicago Press, 1979), 338.

62 Bridges, *Respectable Sins*, 151.

Envy, jealousy, and rivalry see everyone as a competitor, everyone as a threat, and every question as a challenge to my authority. I see these attitudes all too often in my fellow pastors and people in our churches. And I am ashamed to admit that I see these attitudes all too often in myself.

Is There Hope?

What can we do about these sins we hardly ever discuss? Is there any hope for miserable, jealous wretches like us? Yes.

First, we need to understand the truth about ourselves as pastors. Our supposed secret attitudes of envy, jealousy, and hate are open scandals before the holy God. But by the power of the indwelling Holy Spirit, you may grow in grace. And that is what we as pastors need. With each episode of sinful jealousy, we will have the option of confessing that sinful attitude and seeking to become more like Christ and less like the demons (Jas 3:16).

The true Christian is able to deal honestly with himself or herself. He or she can truthfully admit that *nobody* can do *everything*. So when someone is better than you at something, you can admit that this is not a surprise. And if they are better at something extremely important to you, then you should gulp hard and carefully admit:

- God created me as I am (Ps 139:14–16, John 3:27).
- God gave me a certain family and set of experiences and giftedness, and I will choose to accept his calling for me as a pastor (Ps 75:6–7, Rom 12:3, 1 Cor 4:7).
- I will choose to accept his calling for that other person / pastor and I will humbly affirm my strengths and equally admit my weaknesses.
- Finally, I admit that it is a sin to compare myself to others, and I choose, by the grace and power of God, to stop with the uncontrolled resentment, insecurities, and fears.

Jealousy, envy, and pride are not merely dandruff of the soul. They are ugly sins. You must guard against them with a serious and determined vigilance, and you must sincerely repent of them when they ooze into your attitudes and threaten to pollute your soul.

9

Secret Sins of Pastors

MANY CHURCHES ARE IN trouble. Often (though certainly not always) the cause is to be laid at the feet of those in positions of leadership. Entrusted with shepherding the souls of men and women and boys and girls, some spiritual leaders sadly give in to secret sins that harm the church in a most insidious way.

There are those whose fall is tragic and public. Their moral failure is devastating, and the effects are staggering. Everyone can feel the disgust of the scandal, and no one is blind to the consequences. Those cannot be considered secret sins of spiritual leaders.

But secret sins do exist and can destroy a church even as the more scandalous transgressions do. I refer to those less obvious, but equally treacherous, sins in this chapter. I also refer to more than the secret sins of pastors, although they must certainly be addressed, because the spiritual leadership in a church also includes the elders, deacons, wives of those in leadership, Sunday school teachers, children's ministry leaders, youth ministry leaders, church musicians, and Bible study teachers. All of these are spiritual leaders in a church, and they too can yield to secret sins which become like termites that eat away from within. What are some of the secret sins of spiritual leaders?

Impatience

God is the God of patience (Rom 15:5), and the Holy Spirit produces this godly character quality in genuine believers who obey the Word and yield themselves to him (Gal 5:22–23). Patience is one of the marks of older, mature, godly men (Titus 2:2), and God commanded that patience be demonstrated by all Christians toward all people (1 Thess 5:14). As spiritual leaders in local churches deal with the flock of God, they need patience in their responses toward people. It's a sin to bully people, to be impatient, combative, or argumentative. But spiritual leaders also need to wait patiently for God to work in his way regarding various ministry situations.

Impatience is a subtle sin that shows an unwillingness to wait for God to act in his time. Leaders often are guilty of leading where God is not directing and in the timing not of his choosing. Local church leaders sometimes forget to wait for God to do His work in His way in His time. Sometimes impatience drives leaders to abandon a ministry before God has, and their impatience can harm the congregation of God.

Manipulation

Related to impatience, the sin of manipulation is another attempt to get your own way in your own time by self-directed means. Through clever thinking and quick wits, many leaders assemble a complicated series of conversations, meetings, and smaller decisions designed to assert their will. But if things begin to go in a direction not planned or not intended, leaders who lack integrity seek to control the outcome by disingenuous comments and behavior to redirect the group. The manipulative leader will be inconsistent in what he says, varying his words to fit each conversation, attempting to control the listener(s).

Different from influence, manipulation is excessive, crafty, and dishonest. Sadly, manipulation is often more present in local churches than honest discussion, gentle persuasion, and biblical assent.

Fearfulness

The attraction to popularity, approval, and success leaves a leader vulnerable to fear and insecurity. Fear of what men say, fear of disapproval, and fear of failure can subtly choke those in spiritual leadership and leave them paralyzed. There's no feeling so free as the freedom from intimidation because you've made the prior commitment to fear God, seeking to please him in everything. As Paul asked the Galatians, "For am I now seeking the approval of man, or of God? Or am I trying to please man? If I were still trying to please man, I would not be a servant of Christ." (Gal 1:10).

One older Irish pastor I met had the lyrics to the old hymn "Courage Brother, Do Not Stumble," written by Scottish pastor Norman Macleod, inscribed on the flyleaf of his Bible. The second stanza possesses such wise words regarding pastoral ministry:

Some will love you,

Some will hate you,

Some will flatter,

Some will spite.

Cease from man and look above,

Trust in God and do the right.

Covetousness

Few churches have large financial resources held in reserve. Most churches live frugally, even from offering to offering. One secret sin of those in spiritual leadership is coveting other churches that have more people, bigger budgets, larger staffs, or newer buildings. Covetousness can bring ruin to the man or woman who yields to its temptation and can also drive churches to "keep up with the neighbors" and fashion ministries based on what everyone else is doing rather than on how God leads them in his Word. In the Old Testament, the nation of Israel frequently made disastrous decisions because they coveted their neighbors and wanted to be like them. This secret sin can bring very obvious, and very sad, consequences to churches today as well.

Inability to Admit Mistakes

Every leader will make mistakes and errors of judgment. Wise leaders learn from their mistakes and humbly communicate to those who follow. But unfortunately, there are some people in positions of spiritual leadership who damage ministries by their inability to accept blame and admit an error. They stubbornly exacerbate their mistake and frustrate the people with this subtle sin.

Regarding dealing with mistakes and admitting errors of judgment, J. Oswald Sanders wrote,

> Spirituality does not guarantee infallible judgment. The Spirit-filled person is less likely to make mistakes of judgment than his secular counterpart, but perfection eludes us all, whatever our level of spiritual development. Even the apostles made mistakes that required divine correction. Spiritual leaders who have given such a significant share of their lives to knowing God, to prayer, and to wrestling with the problems of renewal and revival may find

it difficult to concede the possibility of misjudgment or mistake. Surely the leader must be a person of strength and decisiveness, to stand for what he believes. But willingness to concede error and to defer to the judgment of one's peers increases one's influence rather than diminishes it. Followers will lose confidence in a leader who appears to believe himself to be infallible. It is strange but true that a perception of infallibility in one area of life often coexists with great humility in other areas.[63]

Suspicion

Discernment is a godly character quality to be sought and honored. It is commended in the Bereans, who searched the Scriptures to find out whether Paul was indeed teaching the truth (Acts 17:11). Discernment is also given major treatment in Proverbs as an important aspect of wisdom.

However, discernment must be controlled by the Word of God and the Spirit of God, or else it can become an attitude of suspicion that casts doubts upon other people's motives and twists them into incorrect conclusions. We must be careful not to project onto others our sinful behaviors, insecurities, attitudes, and motives ("I know what I'd do in that situation . . . and so that must be what they're doing!") Also, note what Cardinal Richelieu, who led the bitter persecution of French Protestants in the seventeenth century, is supposed to have said: "Give me six lines written by the most honorable of men, and I will find an excuse in them to hang him."[64] It is indeed grievous when this type of spirit is found in people in our congregation or in our spiritual leaders.

To assume the worst in people is a burdensome type of leadership that is not loving, godly leadership. Instead, love rejoices in the truth (discernment), bears all things, believes all things, and hopes all things (not suspicious) (1 Cor 13:6–7). The Spirit-controlled balance we should seek is discernment and love as opposed to the natural attitude of suspicion. Suspicious leaders wreak havoc in local church relationships.

---

63 J. Oswald Sanders, *Spiritual Leadership* (Chicago: Moody, 1994), 156- 157.

64 As quoted in *The Cyclopedia of Practical Quotations* (1896) by Jehiel Keeler Hoyt, 763.

Pride

When people rise in position and authority, the natural tendency is for pride to arise. And if unconfessed or undeterred, pride will lead to destruction because "God resists the proud" (Jas 4:6, 1 Pet 5:5). Pride in spiritual leaders takes many forms—an unwillingness to delegate, a prayerless life of furious activity done in the strength of the flesh, an unteachable attitude, or a desire to protect "my turf, my territory, my programs, my office, and my ideas." Pride is seen when leaders cling to their positions in ministry with the notion of indispensability, or when they begin to believe their way is always the better way.

Nothing poses a greater peril for spiritual leaders than our tendency toward exaggerated opinions of self-worth. God will not only remove his blessing from the proud but also actively resist them. That is devastating.

Conclusion

There are scandalous sins that no one would deny will bring ruin to a church, but secret sins can also destroy. May we commit ourselves to be men of God who do not allow our subtle, secret sins to become termites that eat away our churches from within.

PERSPECTIVES ON NURTURING THE FLOCK

10

Expository Preaching

I AM CONVINCED THAT TO nurture and grow healthy congregations, pastors and churches must remain steadfast in their commitment to expository teaching and preaching of the Word of God. While some churches have diminished the value of the Bible—and others have all but abandoned preaching—expository preaching must remain a defining mark of Christ-honoring, biblically grounded churches.

In an age where worship is often reduced to a therapeutic experience, we must boldly reaffirm this truth: strong, vibrant churches are built on the faithful, systematic proclamation of Scripture. The church must regularly renew its dedication to preaching that is rooted in the text, shaped by sound doctrine, and aimed at spiritual transformation.

The definition of expository preaching comes from the Latin word where we get the English word "expose." An expository sermon exposes, reveals, or opens up the meaning of a specific passage of Scripture. The expositor opens up the Bible and explains what it means, thus exposing its meaning.

The Sufficiency of Scripture in the Old Testament

The reason for my commitment to expository preaching is simple—I believe in the sufficiency of Scripture.

In the Old Testament, we read the testimony of Psalm 19:7–19. Note the following statements about the sufficiency of Scripture from this passage. Scripture is

- perfect (literally complete or sufficient),
- sure (trustworthy, reliable, unmovable like a firm foundation),

- right (correct path for life),
- pure (radiant, clear, lucid and not confusing, puzzling, or mystifying),
- clean (not susceptible to decay, not corrupt, but pure, never to be outdated),
- true (able to sanctify as in John 17:17).

Scripture alone has the power to transform the soul, impart wisdom, bring lasting joy, foster deep understanding, and produce genuine righteousness. No therapeutic platitudes, deistic philosophies, or merely inspirational messages can accomplish all that. Neither can talks that only superficially reference God or Scripture. Only sermons firmly grounded in the truth of the Bible can truly achieve life-changing results.

Similar testimony regarding the sufficiency of Scripture is found in that lengthy, glorious passage in Psalm 119. Continually, God affirms throughout all 176 verses of Psalm 119 that his Word is sufficient.

The Sufficiency of Scripture in the New Testament

The New Testament provides similar testimony to the supernatural power of the Bible. In 2 Timothy 3:16 it reads, "All Scripture is breathed out by God and profitable (*ōphelimos*)," or another translation would read "sufficient." Verse 16 continues by declaring that Scripture is sufficient in these ways:

- to teach (*didaskalian*) the doctrinal truth of God,
- to expose (*elegmon*) sinful conduct and erroneous teaching,
- to correct (*epanorthōsin*) straighten up, lift up behavior,
- to train (*paideian*) child rearing, nurturing in righteousness from spiritual infancy to spiritual maturity.

There is a purpose for the Scriptures as seen in verse 17: "that the man of God may be complete, equipped for every good work." God gave us the Bible to reveal himself in an authoritative, accurate revelation so that we would be transformed, not merely informed. I am committed to expository preaching because I am committed to equipping God's people for every good work he has appointed for them.

There is another reason for my commitment to expository preaching: God's Word is alive (Heb 4:12). This means the Bible is not what God would say if he were here today, but what God is saying because he is here today in his living Word. And the power of his sufficient Word is seen in Hebrews 4:13. The Greek word translated "open" in that verse was used of criminals who were being led to trial or execution with the point of a dagger under their chin. Scripture forces us to see who we truly are in God's estimation.

The Conviction in Expository Preaching

Expository preaching begins with a conviction, not a method. The conviction is that the Bible's words are to be explained clearly, carefully, and accurately. An expositor is solemnly bound to say what God says. In an expository message we relate precisely what a text of Scripture says. The Bible passage must determine the substance of the expository sermon. "In many sermons the biblical passage read to the congregation resembles the national anthem played at a football game—it gets things started but is not heard again during the afternoon."[65]

The conviction about the primacy of the Bible must dominate the expository preacher. As John Stott has written,

> Whether the Bible text is long or short, our responsibility as expositors is to open it up in such a way that it speaks its message clearly, plainly, accurately, relevantly without addition, subtraction, or falsification. In expository preaching the biblical text is neither a conventional introduction to a sermon on a largely different theme, nor a convenient peg on which to hang a ragbag of miscellaneous thoughts, but a master which dictates and controls what is said.[66]

The Process in Expository Preaching

The right attitude must be followed by the right method: sound exegesis of the text with attention to historical, grammatical, literal interpretation, all of which means diligent study. This involves hard work and preparation led by the Holy Spirit. The process in expository preaching could be summarized this way:

- The preacher as student searches the truth ("study," Ezra 7:10)

---

65 Haddon Robinson, *Biblical Preaching* (Grand Rapids: Baker Academic, 3rd edition, 2014), 20.

66 John Stott, *Between Two Worlds* (Grand Rapids: Wm. B Eerdmans, Reprint edition, 2017), 126.

- The preacher as disciple applies the truth to himself ("obey," Ezra 7:10)
- The preacher as teacher proclaims the truth ("teach," Ezra 7:10)

John MacArthur puts it this way: "preaching the Bible expositionally carries with it the mandate of diligent study. Fruitful expository preaching demands great effort."[67] Jay Adams similarly identifies what he believes is the number one reason for poor preaching:

> I have had the opportunity to hear much preaching over the last few years, some good, some mediocre, most very bad. What is the problem with preaching? There is no one problem, of course.... But if there is one thing that stands out most, perhaps it is the problem I mention today. What I am about to say may not strike you as being as specific as other things I have written, yet I believe it is at the bottom of a number of other difficulties. My point is that good preaching demands hard work. From listening to sermons and from talking to hundreds of preachers about preaching, I am convinced that the basic reasons for poor preaching is the failure to spend adequate time and energy in preparation. Many preachers—perhaps most—simply don't work long enough on their sermons.[68]

Note what 2 Timothy 2:15 commands: "Do your best to present yourself (*parastēsai*) to God as one approved, a worker who has no need to be ashamed, rightly handling (*orthotomounta* cutting straight) the word of truth." The pastor is to be a diligent workman (hard laborer), who cuts straight the Word of God (with precision), and this kind of ministry is "approved by God." My goal as a pastor must be to craft biblically accurate sermons through careful study, and then communicate the truth from God's Word so that the Holy Spirit will take his Word and supernaturally accomplish his work in the hearts, minds, and souls of the listeners ... because one day God will inspect my work.

But we pastors are constantly pressured:

---

67 John MacArthur, *Preaching: How to Preach Biblically* (Nashville: Thomas Nelson, 2021), 171.

68 Jay Adams, "Editorial: Good Preaching Is Hard Work," *The Journal of Pastoral Practice* (4:2, 1980).

- To give in to market-driven philosophy, where preaching is minimized (I never want my preaching to be merely a form of therapy as a moralistic feel-good theology).
- To underestimate the awesome power of God's Word and God's Spirit (I never want to lose the sense of the supernatural in my ministry).
- To quit because of discouragement (because I'm "not seeing any results").
- To neglect disciplined study (I need to sit at my desk until the hard work is done).

An Expositor Is Not a Dictionary

Preaching is a living process involving the truth of God, the Spirit of God, the man of God, and the people of God. But many people have squirmed for hours listening to lifeless explanations from a preacher-as-dictionary who is as dry as dust. Such preaching misses the point of God's Word. God gave us the Bible to change lives and bring us into conformity to Jesus Christ!

An expository sermon is not just commenting on a book of the Bible, verse by verse, and then moving to another book of the Bible and repeating the process. An expository sermon is not simply a verse-by-verse definition of Hebrew and Greek words, explaining every tense and every verb and every definition, and then concluding. An expository sermon must both explain *and* apply God's truth. It must appeal both to the mind *and* to the heart in an attempt to capture the will. Warren Wiersbe notes,

> I fear that our "cerebral preaching" has created a church composed of people who have big heads but small hearts. The sanctuary has become a lecture hall and too many people are more concerned with filling their notebooks with outlines than filling their hearts with God's love.... As I hear the Word of God, unless a connection takes place between my mind and heart, I won't grow in a balanced way.[69]

---

69 Warren Wiersbe, *Preaching & Teaching with Imagination* (Grand Rapids: Baker Books, 1997), 312.

The Issue of Perspicuity and Preaching

The word perspicuity means "clarity." The doctrine of perspicuity is a crucial doctrine for preaching. It means that the message of the Bible is clear and understandable and that the Bible can be properly interpreted in a normal, literal sense and comprehended even by the uneducated.

The doctrine of the perspicuity of Scripture was a main belief of the Reformers. Martin Luther taught against the Roman Catholic Church's claim that the Bible is too obscure and difficult for common people to understand. The priests and bishops taught the Bible was unclear, and people should not be trusted to interpret or even read it for themselves. In direct contrast, the Reformers taught that God communicates his written revelation to all men, even the unlettered, and they encouraged lay Christians to study and interpret God's Word on their own. They believed the Bible was inherently clear. Because they believed in the perspicuity of Scripture, men such as Wycliffe, Tyndale, and Luther went to great lengths (facing violent opposition, even death, from Catholic leaders) to translate the Bible into the vernacular.

The doctrine of perspicuity applies to our preaching as well. As the Bible is clear and understandable, so should our sermons be clear and understandable. The average listener should be able to perceive how your sermon is structured, with clear order and arrangement, always pointing back to and explaining the biblical text.

The preacher who has truly mastered the text is able to communicate it in such a way that others grasp what he is saying. Therefore, the preacher must be coherent and logical before he is fervent and passionate. I like how Albert Martin explains it: "We must labor to present God's Word in such a way that no reasonably intelligent and careful listener, adult or child, could fail to discern where we began, what path we took, and where we arrived as our destination."[70]

One local church elder lamented the reality that many preachers are incoherent and unclear:

> As a businessman, I've been in Rotary for almost thirty years, and every month we have a meeting and someone gives a talk of some sort. When I go home, I can tell my wife what the talk was about, and how the person made his point. But I can rarely do that with

---

[70] Albert N. Martin, *The Man of God. His Preaching and Teaching Labors* (Montville, NJ: Trinity Pulpit, 2019), 52.

sermons. I think we should shut the theological seminaries down and send our [pastoral] candidates to Rotary International.[71]

These words are such a sad indictment and should startle all seminaries and preachers! Pastor, your prayer should be that your sermons always reflect the perspicuity of Scripture and are careful expositions of the Scripture.

A New Resolve to Preaching

Occasionally, pastors hear whispers from disgruntled people in the pew: "I'm not being fed," or "I prefer that church and preacher over there to ours." Such words and sentiments strike deeply into the heart of every preacher, which is often why the words are whispered in the first place.

But as painful as it is for me to admit, not every sermon of mine has been equally dynamic and soul-riveting. I know there have been times when I could have done a better job on prayerful, diligent sermon preparation. Maybe I really didn't feed the people like I should have on that Sunday. How can we as preachers deal with this?

I think the only way is to be determined to be prayed up and studied up the next time you're in the pulpit. Resolve to get up early each day the next week and pray as a man of God should. Then study seriously. Grapple with next Sunday's text. Turn off the television. Stop surfing the web. Put away your fantasy team rosters. Dig into the Bible. Pull off from your shelves those theology books and commentaries of yours and pore over them. Review your old Bible college/seminary class lecture notes. Accept the challenge of that passage you'll be preaching, and wrestle with its meaning, outline, and application.

Approach next Sunday with all the earnestness you can. After all, it's God's holy and written Word you are handling! Get serious about it once again, like you did when you first began preaching. Shake off the cobwebs and preach with fire in your soul, accepting the calling from God to be the spokesman to your people in your congregation for him. Let them see his glory through you as you seriously handle his words. And don't be afraid of being appropriately direct and bold, assuming nothing with respect to the spiritual condition of the individuals in your congregation. Preach with the authority of God, bearing God's message, speaking God's Word, and forgetting about yourself and your own authority.

---

71 T. David Gordon, *Why Johnny Can't Preach* (Phillipsburg, NJ: P&R Publishing, 2009), 21.

It was the seventeenth-century English Puritan pastor Richard Baxter who wrote, "I preached as never sure to preach again, and as a dying man to dying men." Baxter first published this couplet as part of his poetry book, which was 173 pages long and its introduction dated: "London: At the Door of Eternity, August 7, 1681." Yet he lived ten more years and was imprisoned twice for his zeal and uncompromising stand as a nonconformist against the Church of England. Baxter is a great example of a man captured by holy zeal, preaching every sermon as if it were his last, because with his poor health and the nation's government against him, it indeed may have been his final sermon.

If you knew next Sunday would be the last sermon you would ever deliver, how would you approach your prayer time and your study time this week? Why not approach *every Sunday* the same way? Then, if the critics still whisper, you can face them with your head held high, knowing before God you've done your best. You know those whispers are *their* problem before God, not *yours*. And that's a liberating feeling.

11

The Priority of Prayer

THE CHRISTIAN LIFE IS made up of so many important activities, how does a pastor determine the church's top priorities? Local evangelism, global missions, worship, Bible study, discipleship, stewardship, fellowship, serving others, nurturing children in the faith, encouraging strong marriages and family . . . all of these, and many more vital activities, cry out for attention in our churches.

Ultimately, Christian ministry is not about methodology, techniques, strategies, plans, and organizational structures. It is supernatural in nature, dependent on the supernatural power of the Holy Spirit and the written revelation of God. The goal of our ministry is to see people decide to live for Jesus Christ. These people are either unbelievers dead in their sins, held captive by Satan and his *kosmos*, or they are Christians indwelt with the Holy Spirit but still struggling with the remnant flesh, living in the *kosmos* and being tempted every day by Satan and his unseen host of demons. Christian ministry involves a very real supernatural world. That's why the foundation for your ministry must be prayer and Bible teaching! We must never forget that Christian ministry is supernatural in nature.

What activity should be on the top of our church's list of priorities? The apostle Paul gave an answer, and it may surprise you.

Paul's Top Priority for Churches

Paul wrote his first letter to Timothy to explain how the church leaders should function. That theme is demonstrated in 1 Timothy 3:14–15: "I am writing these things to you so that, if I delay, you may know how one ought to behave in the household of God." First Timothy was written to a young pastor by an older, more experienced pastor with instructions on how to lead the local church.

In this letter of instruction, Paul specifically said that the top priority of the church should be prayer: "First of all, then, I urge that supplications, prayers, intercessions, and thanksgiving be made for all people" (1 Tim 2:1). The Greek words translated "first of all" are *prōton pantōn*. And that word *prōton* most often is used in the New Testament to indicate first in rank, first in importance, first in priority (as opposed to first in line, first in sequence, or numbering without thought of importance). That word *prōton* indicates priority, and by using that word, Paul gave to Timothy the first priority of the church. The number one priority of a church is to pray.

Obviously, this doesn't mean that a church should only pray. That is clear when we see all the important ministries a church is instructed to do in the New Testament. Some of those vital ministries are listed at the beginning of this chapter.

But 1 Timothy 2:1 means that all of our church ministries should begin with prayer and be sustained by prayer, with a total dependence upon the Lord. First Timothy 2:1 also means that our churches should be known as the place where God's people gather to pray and worship him. In the former Soviet Union, church buildings are called houses of prayer. That is a great reminder for American Christians of what the church's top priority should be.

But Is This the Case?

Would you say that prayer is the top priority for many of our churches? Do you think our churches are placing their top efforts at praying together in church, praying together at home as families, and praying alone at home? In my five decades of experience as a Christian, I can't say this is true. Paul says the number one priority of a church is to pray, yet in so many churches it doesn't even make the top five priorities as demonstrated in actual practice—a staggering indictment of many churches here in America.

I believe we need a renewed emphasis on fervent prayer throughout our churches. If we're not praying fervently in our churches, then we're relying on our strength. And without fervent prayer, churches cease to be vibrant expressions of the living God. They become social clubs devoid of supernatural power. They become the machines of pastors and church leaders, grinding away Sunday after Sunday without the oil of the Holy Spirit. Churches like this are not worth preserving.

Biblical Calls for Prayer

We see in 1 Timothy 2:1 that prayer is to be the church's first priority, but there are also other commands in the Bible regarding prayer. We are to "pray without ceasing" (1 Thess 5:17), which means we should live a lifestyle of dependence on God's power appropriated through prayer. We are to pray persistently (Luke 11:1–13, 18:1–8). We are to pray regularly (Eph 6:18, Phil 4:6, Col 4:2, 12). We are to pray fervently, energetically, and passionately (Jas 4:16).

If we don't pray, we don't have power from on high. He promises to answer (Jer 33:3), but only if we call out to him. Pastor, are you calling on him for power, or are you relying on yourself and your efforts?

Historic Calls for Prayer

Long ago, Oswald Sanders wrote about the need for prayer in the life of every pastor by comparing this need to the ministry of John the Baptist: "Immersed in the oil of the Spirit and touched by the fire of God, his life became incandescent. The secret of his effectiveness lay in the fact that his whole personality was dominated and inter-penetrated by the Holy Spirit."[72] Every pastor should have a tongue ignited with holy fire as the Holy Spirit empowers us through fervent prayer.

There is more to preaching than speaking. There is all the difference in the world between ministering to people from human understanding in human energy and ministering to people after fervent prayer. The most humbling and wonderful experience is to minister knowing God is with you. The most frightening is to feel that you are on your own. As D. Martyn Lloyd-Jones wrote, "There is nothing more terrible for a preacher than to be in the pulpit alone, without the conscious smile of God."[73]

Charles Spurgeon constantly called his students to live holy lives filled with fervent prayer. He wrote, "The sacred anointing upon the preacher, and the divine power applying the truth to the hearer ... these are infinitely more important than any details of manner."[74] As churches, we have the truth of the Bible. But are we fretting over "details of manner" (in Spurgeon's words) and missing the divine power when applying the truth? God help us!

---

72 Oswald Sanders, *Men from God's School* (London: Marshall, Morgan and Scott, 1967), 180.

73 D. Martyn Lloyd-Jones, *Christian Unity: Ephesians 4:1–16* (Grand Rapids: Zondervan), 71.

74 Charles Spurgeon, *Lectures to My Students* (Grand Rapids: Zondervann 1980), 96.

Conclusion

God is jealous for your church's exclusive love, as demonstrated in fervent prayer. Pastors giving only lip service to this highest priority of the church are not worth preserving in their leadership roles. Because prayerless churches are really nothing more than social clubs. And unless they repent, God will cease to smile upon their ministry, which is a tragedy of eternal proportions.

Peter Deyneka, Sr. was the founder of Slavic Gospel Association. In his heavy Russian accent he often reminded people, "Much prayer, much power. Little prayer, little power. No prayer, no power."[75] Those are such simple words, but they express a profound truth that is relevant to all believers in any age. May we recommit ourselves to the priority of prayer!

---

75 Peter Deyneka, Sr., *Much Prayer Much Power* (Loves Park, IL: Slavic Gospel Association, 1999).

12

Balance in Ministry

IN MY MINISTRY, I have spent a tremendous amount of time talking to pastors, pastors' wives, educators, missionaries, chaplains, local church leaders, and local church regular folks. I frequently remind them that we need to represent a biblical balance in our ministries.

What do I mean by balance? Pursuing Christ with great passion while loving people and teaching the truth. Loving God and loving people. Serving to help strengthen the church while also reaching out to the lost. Defending the truth and proclaiming the truth. Praying and trusting God while at the same time working hard. Serving and worshipping and instructing and rejoicing and sympathizing and encouraging and disciplining. All of the above in balance, all at the same time in life and ministry. Balance.

I believe many errors in local churches are not ones of substance, but degree. A pastor can poorly lead his church while teaching wonderful things. How? By giving the good things he does teach disproportionate emphasis in his ministry.

For example, a leader can faithfully articulate the Bible's teaching on evangelism or can emphasize music in worship or prioritize mercy ministry, but do it so strongly and so often that the church loses a sense of balance regarding that teaching. Soon faithfulness in the Christian life is defined by the degree of involvement in evangelism (alone) or music in worship (alone) or mercy ministry (alone). This thinking leads to imbalance.

This concern for imbalance is why earlier in my ministry, with a team of wonderful ministry leaders, we identified twenty-one vital signs of healthy churches.[76] The team I worked with on this project felt compelled to identify

---

76 For ten years, from the mid-1990s through the mid-2000s, the leadership team of IFCA International drafted this list and considered them as organizational goals. These twen-

these vital signs because pastors and churches can get so out of balance that we lose focus of some other vital aspects of the Christian life and church life.

Consider these twenty-one vital signs of healthy churches as a comprehensive assessment tool rather than a hierarchical ranking. Each sign represents an essential aspect of church health that, when properly balanced, creates a vibrant, biblical ministry. While no church achieves perfect equilibrium in all areas, this checklist provides valuable benchmarks for leadership teams to evaluate current ministries, identify areas of disproportionate emphasis, and make strategic adjustments to guide their congregation toward greater balance.

Twenty-one Vital Signs of Healthy and Balanced Churches

1. Doctrinal Purity

    A church that is committed to preserving, defending, and proclaiming the historic, fundamental teachings of the Christian faith as set forth in the Word of God, and a biblical world view as derived from its teachings.

2. God-Centered Worship

    A church that is committed to passionately declaring to the Triune God, in personal devotion and corporate assembly, his infinite value and glory through prayer, praising his name, proclaiming his Word, and delighting in his works.

3. Holy Living

    A church that is committed to pursuing and promoting godly character that begins with the renewing of the mind and motivates biblically moral and ethical conduct resulting in personal integrity.

4. Missions Involvement

    A church that is committed to the global proclamation of the gospel to people of every nation, tribe, ethnic, and language group and the establishment of biblical local churches.

---

ty-one goals were renamed in 2006 as "Vital Signs of Healthy IFCA Churches."

5. Church Extension

    A church that is committed to aggressive involvement in planting, establishing, and nurturing biblical, local churches in the United States of America.

6. Expository Preaching

    A church that is committed to effective communication in preaching that emphasizes sound exegesis, historical, grammatical, literal interpretation, with relevant application.

7. Relevant Teaching

    A church that is committed to accuracy and appropriate creativity in the teaching of God's Word, enabling people to understand and apply God's truth, and to develop a consistent world view.

8. Fervent Prayer

    A church that is committed to the practice and promotion of both private and corporate prayer.

9. Leadership Development

    A church that is committed to identifying and preparing successive generations of leaders to lead the church into the future.

10. Servant Leadership

    A church that is committed to the development of leaders who reflect the selflessness of Christ in the leadership of those to whom they minister.

11. Intentional Equipping

    A church that is committed to facilitating the development of spiritual gifts and ministry skills among all its members, encouraging each one to be a fully functioning minister in the local body.

12. Evangelistic Zeal

    A church that is compelled by the love of Christ, and therefore is committed to the passionate proclamation of the gospel to all people, because all men apart from Christ are lost and face the horrors of eternal judgment.

13. Compassionate Concern

    A church that is committed to recognizing and responding to the physical, material, and emotional needs of both Christians and non-Christians in such a way as to bring them the touch of God's love and compassion as well as the light of his redemption.

14. Biblical Separation

    A church that is committed to biblical separation and church discipline exercised with a humble, gracious spirit and applied in such a way as to strengthen the body of Christ.

15. Multi-Generational Ministry

    A church that is committed to ministries which will reach, teach, equip, and involve people of all ages and groups (men, women, boys, and girls) so that we may present everyone complete in Christ.

16. Multi-Cultural / Ethnically Diverse Ministry

    A church that is seeking to reflect the ethnically and culturally blended nature of the body of Christ and is actively fostering the continuing expansion of its ethnic and cultural diversity.

17. Unified Purpose

    A church that is committed to the pursuit of unity in the advancement of a common cause.

18. Effective Communication

    A church that is committed to an effective information strategy to clearly, thoughtfully, and sensitively distribute useful data.

19. Biblical Conciliation

    A church that is committed to biblical unity and resolving any episodes of disharmony among believers in a Christ-honoring fashion.

20. Financial Stewardship

    A church that is committed to biblical principles of generosity and integrity in the stewardship of financial resources and the teaching of such principles to the congregation.

21. Continual Improvement

    A church that recognizes the lordship of Christ in the totality of life and is committed to the regular reassessment of its methodology, activities, and vision regarding their effectiveness for the glory of God.

The Goal of Balance

Those twenty-one vital signs of healthy churches seem impossible to balance. However, it should always be the goal of every believer in the local church to be like our Savior, reflecting his balance. What would that look like? What are some of the ways this balance should be seen? Well, I admit that's the difficulty.

I believe that balance in the life of an individual believer will reflect the character qualities produced by the indwelling Holy Spirit as listed in Galatians 5:22–23 (love, joy, peace, patience, kindness, goodness, faithfulness, meekness, self-control). And men of balance will exhibit the qualities described in 1 Timothy 3; women of balance will reflect the qualities in Proverbs 31. Also, both men and women of balance will reflect the qualities in Titus 2.

In the local church, how do we pastors achieve a Bible-balanced ministry? Again, the answer isn't a simple one, but I believe the key is to consistently preach the themes of Scripture in proper relationship to one another. In other words, pastors should aim to preach what the Bible says, in the way it says it, to the degree it says it. And if you do that consistently enough, long enough, and model balance in your own personal life, the church will start reflecting balance in its ministries and in the lives of the members of the congregation.

And if our churches are filled with individuals whose lives are balanced, with a pastor whose teaching ministry reflects balance, then ours will be healthy churches.

13

The Pastor and Biblical Counseling

Throughout church history, pastors have sought to help people obey the Word of God in their daily lives as people have properly sought spiritual counsel from pastors. It has always been a vital part of the ministry of a pastor to provide counsel according to God's Word. The purpose of the Bible-based pastor should be to counsel each individual to become more conformed to the image of Jesus Christ, with a Godward focus in every aspect of life (Rom 8:28–29).

The same God who saves us from everlasting destruction also brings us into a life that exemplifies his grace here on earth. There is profound transformational power in the life of a regenerated Christian through the work of the indwelling Holy Spirit (Gal 5:16–23) and through the living Word of God (Heb 4:12).

The content of biblical counseling should consist of the proclamation of Christ in the gospel and the implications for living that proceed from the gospel. The biblical grounds for counseling are found in verses like these:

- "We who are strong ought have an obligation to bear with the failings of the weak, and not just please ourselves" (Rom 15:1).
- "... instruct [*noutheteō*: counsel, instruct, warn, confront] one another" (Rom 15:14)
- "Brothers, if anyone is caught in any transgression, you who are spiritual should restore him in a spirit of gentleness. Keep watch on yourself, lest you too be tempted. Bear one another's burdens, and so fulfill the law of Christ." (Gal 6:1–2).
- "Therefore encourage one another and build one another up" (1 Thess 5:11)

- "But exhort one another every day, as long as it is called 'today,' that none of you may be hardened by the deceitfulness of sin." (Heb 3:13)
- "Therefore, confess your sins to one another, and pray for one another" (Jas 5:16)

Biblical counseling is built on this simple, enduring principle: the triune God has spoken to us through the Scriptures and enables us to grow in grace through the indwelling Holy Spirit. In the midst of life's battles and hardships, and as we counsel hurting people, Jesus Christ must be the center of all Christian counseling. He is the Creator (Col 1:16), and since he is, then who should know more about the human mind, personality, and behavioral change than the Creator as the master designer?

Second Peter 1:3–4 teaches that God has revealed to us in his Word ("his precious and very great promises") everything we need to know about him, about ourselves, and about the world around us. The Bible shows us what is acceptable behavior and unacceptable behavior, instructs us how to live and how not to live. The Bible presents to us clear commandments and principles for us to follow that teach us how to experience genuine behavioral change. The Bible lays the framework for interpersonal relationships. It gives practical advice on solving family, marital, and personal conflicts. It reveals everything we need for life and godliness.

Second Peter 1:3–4 also teaches that we are "partakers of the divine nature," meaning we have a regenerated (new and holy) nature through the indwelling Holy Spirit. At the moment of regeneration the believer is justified, forgiven, adopted into God's family, and receives a new nature; the Holy Spirit comes to dwell within (1 Cor 6:19, Rom 8:9). And with the indwelling Spirit of God, the believer is given everything needed for life and godliness (2 Pet 1:3). Old things pass away (2 Cor 5:17), and the new believer is translated from the kingdom of darkness into the kingdom of God's Son (Col 1:13), placed onto the pathway of holiness. With the Holy Spirit on the inside giving supernatural power and the Word of God on the outside giving supernatural direction, the believer can be everything God wants him or her to be.

The issue in counseling and spiritual transformation becomes one of authority and power. Who or what has authority? And is there any power to transform lives? For the biblical counselor, the authority and power rests upon the Word of God and the work of the Holy Spirit.

The Bible and Behavior

To counsel from the Bible is to advise, and even more specifically, to direct. Biblical counseling is directive in nature. In other words, counseling is not to be vague but specific and direct.

Biblical counselors do not just act as a "sounding board," but they warn, challenge, give advice, guide, admonish, and even rebuke. That's the meaning behind *noutheteō* in Romans 15:14 "instruct (*noutheteō*) one another." In our human pride, we like to think we have all the answers and our way is the best way. As sinners, we suppress the truth of God (Rom 1:18), and we try to reinterpret the universe on the basis that we as individuals give things and events their meaning. But we need God's Word to confront us with his answers, his way. And confronting humans in their pride and self-will is not easy.

While admittedly the work of counseling is not easy, it's very much needed. It's the process by which one Christian restores another to a place of usefulness to Christ in his church. The command in the Word of God is very clear—we are to "restore" (Gal 6:1) any brothers or sisters God providentially places in our pathway.

The Greek word for "restore" in Galatians 6:1 (*katartizō*) was used by first-century fishermen and physicians when they described the mending of fish nets and the setting of fractures. They both called their work "restoration." A torn net is of little or no value; the fish easily slip through and are lost. Likewise, a broken bone in the arm makes it useless until the broken bone is set. Torn nets and broken arms need to be restored to their former use.

When we counsel, we must seek restoration by asking, "How has this person's usefulness to Christ been diminished by his problem/his sin?" This goal ought to guide our methods, attitudes, and activities in helping the counselee. We counsel not to punish nor to gloat over the person's sins nor to become voyeuristically fascinated with every detail of their sin. Our sole desire is to bring him to usefulness and victory in the Lord (1 Cor 10:31, Col 3:23).

Galatians 6:1 also makes it clear that in restoration there must be the element of compassionate concern and empathy ("restore him in a spirit of gentleness"), or else confrontation will be sterile, lifeless, cold, professional, harsh, and probably done out of a critical spirit. There should be no hint of nastiness or a condescending know-it-all-attitude in the process of confrontation.

True biblical counseling starts with empathy, communicating to people: "Yes, life is bad. Yes, it's normal to hurt. And yes, God knows and understands your hurt." When someone like the great apostle Paul feels the sentence of death in his circumstances (as he did in 2 Cor 1:8), that should instruct us to stop and acknowledge our counselee's pain and empathize with him or her before we rush in with words of correction or attempts to offer quick fixes. That empathy is crucial in biblical counseling.

Elements of Biblical Counseling

Jay Adams noted the following about biblical counseling:

> It contains three elements: change through confrontation out of concern. It presupposes that there are sinful patterns and activities in the life of the counselee that God wants **changed**; that this change will be brought about through a verbal **confrontation** of the counselee with the Scriptures as the counselor ministers to them in the power of the Holy Spirit; and that this confrontation is done in a loving, caring, familial manner for the benefit of the counselee. There is deep **concern**.[77]

Biblical counseling suggests there's something wrong with the person who is to be confronted biblically. Counseling arises out of the fact that there's a condition in his or her life which you can determine (through prayerful listening) that God wants to be changed, based on what the Bible says. The fundamental purpose of nouthetic confrontation is to bring about personality and behavioral change, conforming to the image of Jesus Christ. God wants his children to change and become more like his Son. All biblical counseling aims at this kind of change.

Biblical counselors believe that the primary element of spiritual transformation is not inherent in us as humans but is given to us by God in the form of grace. Grace always propels us towards holiness, goodness, godliness, and righteousness. Without God's grace, authentic change is unattainable.

Biblical counseling may be defined in short as:

1. meeting the person where he is and empathetically listening to his story
2. seeking to find the point(s) of pride and sin in his life

---

[77] Jay Adams, *Ready to Restore—The Layman's Guide to Christian Counseling* (Phillipsburg, NJ: Presbyterian & Reformed Publishing Co., 1992), 9.

3. graciously pointing out what is wrong and unbiblical
4. helping him obtain the desirable behavioral change through his appropriating God's grace
5. all of this process based upon prayer, dependent upon the Holy Spirit and directed by Scripture.

But does biblical counseling work? In the book *Counseling the Hard Cases,* eleven experienced biblical counselors report real-life case studies. Compiled by editors Stuart Scott and Heath Lambert, the introduction states that in the development of the modern biblical counseling movement over the last fifty years, persuasive evidence shows that "Scripture is comprehensively sufficient to do ministry with people experiencing profound difficulties in their lives."[78] Yes, it does work, as you'd assume since the Spirit of God and the Word of God are supernaturally able to accomplish God's purposes.

Life Is Hard

One of the ways God accomplishes the spiritual growth of his children is through refinement by trials and suffering (Jas 1:2–4). And the world is filled with trials and suffering. Sin has affected every aspect of life, especially in the area of human relationships. Misunderstanding, miscommunication, suspicion, unfulfilled expectations, hurtful words, unforgiveness, and sinful selfishness are prevalent in all our relationships.

What are we to do when confronted with hardship and pain in our lives or in the lives of our counselees? The non-Christian world says it's almost hopeless and with an uncertain voice suggests counseling (*"talk it out with a counselor"*) or psychotherapy (*"go to a real expert and dig deep into your thoughts, emotions, and past experiences through extensive psychotherapy"*) or dispense a never-ending supply of psychotropic, mood-altering drugs (*"take this pill and it will make you feel better"*).

But it must be remembered that the Lord Jesus predicted for his followers (even promised us) a hard life: "in the world you **will** have tribulation" (John 16:33). Life in this fallen and broken world has a way of knocking us down with hurts, disappointments, and confusion. I sin against others, others sin against me, and circumstances overwhelm us.

---

[78] Stuart W. Scott and Heath Lambert, eds. *Counseling the Hard Cases* (Nashville: Broadman & Holman, 2012), 23.

All of this means we can understand what the apostle Paul felt in 2 Corinthians 1:8. After telling the Corinthians about the hardships he suffered, Paul admitted that the pressure he experienced seemed to be far more than he could endure. He confessed that in his heart he felt the sentence of death, and he despaired even of life. Yet in these painful circumstances Paul said he learned to trust "on God who raises the dead" (2 Cor 1:9). God was transforming Paul and growing his faith and trust, in the midst of Paul's suffering and pain. And God was doing this by means of his supernatural power that raises the dead.

We shouldn't be surprised by trials and troubles, even in a Christian's life. And we must tell ourselves and everyone we counsel that life is hard. Assuming that God will make life easy is not helpful for spiritual transformation. There is redemptive value in every problem. God can use them for our good, and he is far more concerned about our character than he is in removing the problem.

God Is Good

When counseling people, the pastor must say, "Life is hard, but God is great and good. You can have hope in him." So, taken together, we can say, "It's normal to hurt, but it's possible to hope."

When despairing even of life, what truth about God did Paul emphasize in his own self-counsel in 2 Corinthians 1:8–9? He focused on the fact that God is great and has worked his supernatural power in raising the dead, overpowering even the most hopeless of all earthly circumstances—death. Paul focused on the God of resurrection.

This kind of focus is instructive for us in biblical counseling. We must communicate to our counselees the truth of 2 Corinthians 1:8–9—that life will be hard, and it will sometimes feel like death. But we must never stop there. We must also say—God is good. He's good all the time, even when it may not feel like that. You need to focus on the almighty power of God, on his goodness, and on his good Word, not on your feelings. Trust him, and obey what he says. See him as the God who knows you, who sees you, who cares for you, and who uses the hard things in your life to make you a more Christ-dependent person.

We should remind our counselees that through all the struggles and difficulties of life, God is faithful. We can depend on him to exercise his awesome power in our lives, accomplishing his purposes in and through us, even as we acknowledge that sometimes the trials and pain in our lives won't be resolved until the next life, in eternity.

So we must not look at life from the perspective of this world of time and space, but rather we must acknowledge that some things, perhaps many things, will not make sense until the next life. We must not look at life from an earthly perspective, but we must look at life from God's eternal perspective. When troublesome circumstances crash all around us and people intend things for evil and they harm and hurt us, God weaves all things together for good (Rom 8:28), and he wants to use those circumstances to mold us into the image of his Son (Rom 8:29). In this world we will have trouble, but take heart! Christ has overcome the world (John 16:33). So, focus on Jesus Christ, hope in him, and you can have peace. We should hope in God and always obey his Word. That's good counsel for anyone.

Counseling Believers and Unbelievers

God, who made everything in the universe, interprets the meaning of all things and events. He has given to us his written revelation, which is necessary to explain man's need for salvation and what he expects of man in this life. As humans, we were created in God's image as responsible beings (Gen 1:26–27), and one day every human will stand before God (2 Cor 5:10, Rev 20:11–15) to give an accounting of the things done in this life. And on that great day of accounting, we'll not be able to make excuses before our Creator. This is a sobering reality all too often forgotten by counselees, and it is a truth which must be communicated by biblical counselors regardless of whether the counselee is a professing Christian or not.

When counseling professing believers, biblical counselors recognize the chief aim must be grounded in the doctrine of sanctification, with conformity to the image of Jesus Christ as the central goal. For the believer, the flesh will be the greatest enemy against which he or she must contend in life and in the counseling process (Gal 5:16–21). The believer must constantly be directed back to the Bible (Ps 119:9–11) and the power of the Holy Spirit over the flesh (Gal 5:22–25).

When counseling non-believers, the chief aim must be to evangelize them with the gospel of Christ so that the fundamental change necessary for their lives might occur. Once they experience regeneration and are born again, the indwelling Holy Spirit begins his life-long work of sanctification, and spiritual transformation can begin . . . but only then. Regeneration by the Holy Spirit is a prerequisite for biblical change.

Some Final Thoughts on Counseling

The Bible is the only complete and authoritative source of revealed truth from God, written specifically to provide the answers to man's spiritual problems and the means for man's behavioral changes. It is totally sufficient in these areas.

The purpose of the Bible-based pastor or any spiritual leader in the church (whether male or female) should be to counsel each individual to become more conformed to the image of Jesus Christ, with a Godward focus in every aspect of life.

The same God who saves us from everlasting destruction also brings us into a life that exemplifies his grace here on earth. There is profound transformational power in the life of a regenerated Christian by the work of the indwelling Holy Spirit through the living Word of God. And all of us, as fallen, imperfect people, should thank God.

14

Love, Emotional Intelligence, and People Skills

I WAS TALKING TO A young pastor, and after our lengthy conversation, I commented on his wisdom and warmth. I told him many pastors fail regarding dealing with people (something we often refer to as people skills or emotional intelligence). When I said this statement, the young pastor was surprised and asked me to elaborate further. So I provided him some specific sad examples of ungracious pastors and their interpersonal blunders. At the close of our conversation, he said something quite profound: "That's so strange. Why would you become a pastor if you don't love people?"

That young pastor asked a great question, which summarizes the basis of pastoral interpersonal skills—love. Love is the bottom-line way to define people skills. And the pastor's life must be characterized by love in the same way that Jesus' life was characterized by love.

The pastor needs the ability to interact with people in a friendly way and with courtesy, compassion, and empathy. He needs to be others-oriented as opposed to being self-absorbed or task-driven. He needs to notice people (without looking past them) and look them in the eye and smile. He needs to be able to call the people of his congregation by name as Jesus said a good shepherd does (John 10:3). The pastor must interact with people and ask sincere questions demonstrating concern, communicating both verbally and non-verbally in ways that demonstrate courtesy and love. The pastor needs to be able to listen effectively, handle difficult conversations, discipline his anger, and help resolve conflict. And if he fails at much of the above, *his ministry is hindered, and he may even be fired from his church!*

This is serious because people expect personal interactions with their pastor to be loving and kind. And for good reason, because Christ was the living embodiment of love and grace. He exemplified courtesy and concern for others. He valued people, welcomed them, conversed with them, and ate with them. So is it wrong for people to expect their pastors to reflect Christlikeness in such basic ways as kindness and personal care? If that's not a wrong expectation, then I would like to ask—what do Christlike interpersonal relationship skills look like?

The Bible's Answer

The Bible clearly addresses the question of interpersonal relations. Note just a few passages: "You shall not take vengeance or bear a grudge against the sons of your own people, but you shall love your neighbor as yourself; I am the LORD" (Lev 19:18). Also, "A soft answer turns away wrath, but a harsh word stirs up anger." (Prov 15:1). The New Testament commands us to "be kind to one another" (Eph 4:32). Paul commanded Titus to "to avoid quarreling, to be gentle, to show perfect courtesy for all people" (Titus 3:2).

The pastor is to reflect Christ's love in his personal interactions, and love is described in 1 Corinthians 13:4–7: "Love is patient and kind; love does not envy or boast; it is not arrogant or rude. It does not insist on its own way; it is not irritable or resentful; it does not rejoice at wrongdoing, but rejoices with the truth. Love bears all things, believes all things, hopes all things, endures all things."

Scripture teaches that the natural works of the flesh lead to terrible human relationships filled with hatred, strife, jealousy, fits of anger, rivalries, dissensions, divisions (Gal 5:20). But when we walk in the Spirit, the fruit demonstrated in our lives will be love, joy, peace, patience, kindness, goodness, faithfulness, meekness and self-control (Gal 5:22–23). If a pastor loves Christ and walks in the Spirit, his people skills will grow. That's why our congregations expect pastors to deal with people in love and wisdom—and that's not an unreasonable expectation.

The simple truth is that pastors and their wives want to be loved by their congregations. But I say to pastors and pastors' wives: if you want to be loved by your flock, then you must first love them. Know them. Serve them. Respect them. Laugh with them. Cry with them. If you want to be loved, you have to love others first.

Pastors need to grasp the importance of fostering genuine relationships within their church, skillfully developing and using those networks of interaction. Engaging with people personally is the mark of a wise pastor, for his effectiveness in ministry is shaped by the strength of his bond with those he serves. An hour of personal time with someone in your congregation can have more impact than a dozen sermons. And one hour of personal time most definitely will have an impact on that person's attention the next Sunday when the pastor is preaching.

Ministry takes place in the context of relationships. We don't minister to pews and bricks and books. We minister to people who desperately need to be changed into the image and likeness of Jesus Christ. And what changes people is the truth of God's Word in the context of relationship.

The World's Answer

The leaders of the world know the value of interpersonal skills. The book *How to Win Friends and Influence People* was written by Dale Carnegie. This book was first published in 1936, and it's still in print today. Tens of millions of copies have been sold worldwide, and the book's title has become a familiar catchphrase. Carnegie's premise was that if you want to influence people, then you must win friends.

Although the pastor may chafe at taking advice from Dale Carnegie (*"what does that man have to say to me?"*), I think many pastors could learn a few things from what Carnegie taught. I am committed to the sufficiency of Scripture to counsel pastors in their interpersonal skills. I know Carnegie was not inspired, nor did he attempt to teach from the Bible. He was just a man, sharing practical tips from his experience, and at times he seemed to advocate techniques that may seem manipulative. But from what I've experienced and observed in churches, parsonages, seminaries, and Bible colleges, many pastors could use a little advice from Carnegie if they filter his advice through their own Scriptural worldview.

Below are the four main components of *How to Win Friends and Influence People*, with the sub-sections listed. Look over these chapter headings and consider your interpersonal skills and emotional intelligence by comparison.

Fundamental Techniques in Handling People

>Don't criticize, condemn, or complain.
>
>Give honest and sincere appreciation.
>
>Arouse in the other person an eager want.

Six Ways to Make People Like You

    Become genuinely interested in other people.

    Smile.

    Remember that a person's name is, to that person, the sweetest and most important sound in any language.

    Be a good listener. Encourage others to talk about themselves.

    Talk in terms of the other person's interest.

    Make the other person feel important—and do it sincerely.

Twelve Ways to Win People to Your Way of Thinking

    The only way to get the best of an argument is to avoid it.

    Show respect for the other person's opinions. Never say "You're Wrong."

    If you're wrong, admit it quickly and emphatically.

    Begin in a friendly way.

    Start with questions to which the other person will answer yes.

    Let the other person do a great deal of the talking.

    Let the other person feel the idea is his or hers.

    Try honestly to see things from the other person's point of view.

    Be sympathetic with the other person's ideas and desires.

    Appeal to the nobler motives.

    Dramatize your ideas.

    Throw down a challenge.

Be a Leader: How to Change People without Giving Offense or Arousing Resentment

    Begin with praise and honest appreciation.

    Call attention to people's mistakes indirectly.

    Talk about your own mistakes before criticizing the other person.

    Ask questions instead of giving direct orders.

    Let the other person save face.

    Praise every improvement.

    Give the other person a fine reputation to live up to.

    Use encouragement. Make the fault seem easy to correct.

Make the other person happy about doing what you suggest.

Conclusion

I challenge you to reread the Bible passages above and consider your own people skills, or lack thereof. Ask your wife to read this chapter and tell you the points you need to work on. And since so many of the pastor's interpersonal problems come from his wife's relationships at church, after carefully listening to your wife's input, graciously offer her the points she can work on. See if there's anything both of you can learn from the revealed Word of God and the uninspired advice from Dale Carnegie.

A pastor must be able to engage people warmly, showing courtesy, compassion, and empathy. He should be genuinely others-focused, not self-absorbed or merely task-driven. This means asking sincere questions, listening attentively, and expressing care through both words and actions that reflect love and respect. Neglecting these qualities will hinder his ministry—and could even cost him his position.

No pastor wants that. This is serious.

PERSPECTIVES ON CULTURE AND MINISTRY

15

Defending the Faith

I'VE ALWAYS FOUND IT compelling that in the letter designed to instruct Timothy how to be a pastor of a local church, the first and last words deal with defending the faith. At the epistle's beginning, Paul instructed Timothy to guard the truth in opposition to false teachers (1 Tim 1:3); and at the epistle's ending, Paul commanded Timothy to guard the truth that was committed to his trust (1 Tim 6:20).

In his exhortation to the Ephesian elders, Paul urged them to guard the flock of God from false teachers (Acts 20:28–30). Peter warned against false teachers who would secretly bring in destructive heresies (2 Pet 2:1–3) and mock God's promises (2 Pet 3:3–4); he cautioned his readers to beware and not fall into the error of the wicked (2 Pet 3:17). Jude commanded us to contend earnestly for the faith against false teachers who would attempt to creep into our churches unnoticed (Jude 3–4). And the Lord Jesus taught about the nature of our Adversary who would seek to destroy God's work in the lives of people (Matt 13:19) and to deceive everyone possible through the enemy's implanted agents (Matt 13:36–43).

Defending the faith is an essential part of the ministry of pastors and churches. Some may shrink back from this, but defending the faith is a rapidly growing reality that every one of our churches must face today. Look at the threats spinning out of control all around us today. There are theological threats we need to defend against:

- Inerrancy questions against the Bible and denials of the historicity of the Bible's accounts
- Denials of eternal retribution and the growing embrace of universalism

- Social justice's growing primacy over gospel centered evangelism
- Mysticism, aberrant and extreme views on the Holy Spirit, the Prosperity Gospel
- The Road Back to Roman Catholicism or Eastern Orthodoxy for misled Protestants
- Churchless Christianity in favor of fellowship at coffee shops and on iPads

And sadly, there are many more.

There are cultural threats we need to defend against:

- Ignorant welcoming of radicalized Islam
- Embracing Postmodernism, rejecting authoritative propositions in favor of relativism, seeking hyper-tolerance, capitulating to atheism
- Surrendering to the aggressive LGBTQ agenda
- Swallowing the philosophies of Pragmatism, Humanism, Consumerism, Hedonism
- Sliding toward Gomorrah with the family under attack through a porn saturated culture, divorce, violence, and radical feminization

And sadly, there are many more.

It seems as though our Western cultures are descending into a new Dark Age, and whether we like it or not, we need to present a vigorous defense of the Christian faith. But what exactly do I mean by defending the faith?

What Does It Mean to Defend?

I believe defending the faith and presenting the gospel are two different activities, but they're inextricably intertwined and will often happen at the same time. Yet you've probably heard it said that a Christian should never argue with an unbeliever, especially when trying to lead the unbeliever to a saving knowledge of Jesus Christ. Is that a correct understanding of evangelism and defending the faith?

If by "argue" you mean sarcastically hurling insulting putdowns and invectives as the star of your own viral podcast, then absolutely, that is most definitely not what you should do when defending the faith or sharing the gospel. The Lord Jesus never stooped to such debating tactics even when he was most shamefully treated, mocked, and murdered. Peter says that when Christ "was reviled, he did not revile in return; when he suffered, he did not threaten, but continued entrusting himself to him who judges righteously" (1 Pet 2:23). Isaiah prophesied this about Messiah: "He was oppressed and he was afflicted, **yet He opened not His mouth**; like a lamb that is led to the slaughter, and like a sheep before its shearers is silent, **so He opened not His mouth**" (Isa 53:5,7, emphasis added). Paul commanded Timothy that "the Lord's servant must not be quarrelsome but kind to everyone, able to teach, patiently enduring evil" (2 Tim 2:24). Arguing with unbelievers in the sense of exchanging loud and angry words is never a godly activity!

If you go to any dictionary, however, you'll see two senses behind the definition of the word argue. One idea is what is presented above: "to exchange or express diverging or opposite views, typically in a heated or angry way" with synonyms such as "quarrel, squabble, bicker, fight."

But the second idea for argue is something totally different: "give reasons or cite evidence in support of an idea, action, or theory, typically with the aim to persuade others to share one's view" with synonyms such as "contend, assert, maintain, insist, hold, allege, reason." We aren't to quarrel and fight with unbelievers by using angry words, but we must seek to persuade them, even debate their ideas, by reasoning with them from the Bible.

Jesus did. He debated with the Sadducees about the resurrection (Matt 22:23–32). He debated with the Herodians about paying taxes to Caesar (Matt 22:16–22). He debated with the Pharisees about the person of the Messiah (Matt 22:41–46). He reasoned with Nicodemus about how to get to heaven (John 3:1–21). He reasoned with a Samaritan woman about true worship (John 4:7–26). If Jesus is our example, we should reason and debate with unbelievers. Now, you may say that Jesus is also God, and we are not. Perhaps only God should debate with unbelievers?

But note that Paul debated with unbelievers. He debated and reasoned with his fellow Jewish people over whether Jesus was the Messiah predicted in the Old Testament (Acts 13:14–43). He debated with the Gentiles and asserted that God demanded they repent from idolatry and worship the One True God (Acts 14:15–18; 17:16–32). If Paul is our example, we too should reason and debate with unbelievers. Of course, Paul was an apostle, and we are not. Perhaps only apostles should debate with unbelievers?

But note that elders are to debate with unbelievers. Paul told Titus that an elder should "hold firm to the trustworthy word as taught, so that he may be able to give instruction in sound doctrine and also to rebuke refute those who contradict it" (Titus 1:9). Presumably, this is the way that church leaders must silence the rebellious men, empty talkers and deceivers (Titus 1:10–11). Of course, not all of us are elders. Maybe only elders should debate with unbelievers?

Peter, however, wrote that all believers should reason and debate with unbelievers. Speaking to Christians, he wrote in 1 Peter 3:15, "in your hearts honor Christ the Lord as holy, always being prepared to make a defense to anyone who asks you for a reason for the hope that is in you; yet do it with gentleness and respect." Therefore, each believer is to prepare himself or herself to be able to debate effectively and reason carefully with those who are unsaved, praying that indeed the Lord may grant them repentance leading to the knowledge of the truth (2 Tim 2:25).

By "defense" I mean a careful explanation of the Bible, clearing away the misrepresentations of those people and philosophies that attack the truth presented in Scripture. I also mean by giving a reasoned defense that we should present what the Bible says regarding any given issue, demonstrating God's thoughts on the issue, letting the Bible defend itself (the self-witness of Scripture). The Bible is the self-authenticating, written revelation of God. This means that the demonstration of the Bible's authenticity is internal to it and externally verified by the Holy Spirit in the hearts and minds of the readers or listeners. As has often been said, you don't defend a lion, you just turn it loose. That's what I mean by defense—just turn the Bible loose by careful, accurate, and patient teaching.

Biblical View of Man

Ultimately, the issue of defending the faith becomes an issue of biblical anthropology—how do you view man? Is he able to comprehend and judge facts as though the fall (Gen 3) had no effect upon him?

To answer this question, you need to understand what the Bible says about humanity. God created everything in the universe, and his imprint is seen everywhere in creation because everything came from his hand. But Romans 1:18–23 teaches that man's problem is not a lack of evidence. Man's problem instead is the cognitive, moral deficiency to interpret what he sees correctly. Romans 1:18–23 says that man suppresses the truth displayed in creation (natural revelation) and rejects its message of God's eternal power and divine nature so that all men are without excuse (Rom 1:20). Unbelieving humans reject what creation reveals to them.

As humans in their unregenerate condition suppress God's natural revelation in creation, we do the same to God's special, written revelation when we twist it and reject it. So you don't take the unregenerate man in his cognitive, moral deficiency and tell him to make judgments on the Bible. You don't offer an unbeliever the authority to judge the veracity of Scripture because this implies that he inherently knows what God can or cannot reveal. The Scriptures are not on trial by the sinner; the sinner is on trial by the Bible.

When you turn the Bible loose, you do so knowing that the unbeliever will at first resist it, twist it, and reject it. But you still patiently and carefully explain what the Bible teaches, hoping and praying that God will open his or her eyes to the truth. When observing God's natural revelation in creation or when reading his written, special revelation in Scripture, there is no neutral fact; a person either accepts the truth or rejects it. Sinners' only hope is if the Holy Spirit illumines their eyes and removes their blindness so they can see the light, the truth of God's revelation.

Balance Between Defending and Trusting

When defending the faith, we must seek a proper balance between defending and trusting. By this statement, I mean we need to defend the faith vigorously while at the same time trusting God to open the unbeliever's eyes to the truth we're explaining from God's Word. We must defend the truth while trusting God to work through his Word and his Spirit to save the unbeliever we are talking to, but this is a difficult balance to achieve.

A number of years ago J. I. Packer wrote a landmark book entitled *Evangelism and the Sovereignty of God*. He was seeking this balance I'm referring to.

> If we regarded it as our job, not simply to present Christ, but actually to produce converts—to evangelize, not only faithfully, but also successfully—our approach to evangelism would become pragmatic and calculating. We should conclude that our basic equipment, both for personal dealing and for public preaching, must be twofold. We must have not merely a clear grasp of the meaning and application of the gospel, but also an irresistible technique for inducing a response. We should, therefore, make it our business to try and develop such a technique. . . . We should not regard evangelism as an activity involving a battle of wills between ourselves and those to whom we go, a battle in which victory depends on our firing off a heavy enough barrage of calculated effects.[79]

---

79 J. I. Packer, *Evangelism and the Sovereignty of God* (Downers Grove, IL: Inter Varsity, 1976), 27–28.

Packer is saying that it's right to engage unbelievers and seek to demonstrate from Scripture where they are incorrect. It's right to desire their conversion. It's right to seek to present the gospel in as clear and intellectually forceful way as possible. But it's wrong "when we take on ourselves more than God has given us to do."[80] You must not take the weight of decision making of unbelievers upon your shoulders by seeking to overpower them intellectually or coerce them, but you must do everything in your power to persuade them, to induce their comprehension of God's claims in the Bible. You must defend the faith.

Implications

Theological and cultural threats are spinning out of control all around us today. We are called to defend the faith, to give reasons and cite evidence from the Bible with the aim of persuading others to agree with what God has written. We are to contend, assert, maintain, insist, hold, allege, and reason from the Scriptures.

Some may shrink back from this call, but defending the faith is not only a Scriptural command but is also a rapidly growing reality that our churches must face today. And all the while we defend the faith, we must trust God the Spirit to open the eyes of unbelievers to the truths of his written revelation.

Defending the faith is an essential part of the ministry of pastors and churches.

---

80 Packer, *Evangelism*, 29.

16

Forgetting the Doctrine of Separation

THIS IS A CALL to purity and balance, representing that truth of God's Word which has fallen upon the rocks of neglect in today's American Church. Such teaching from the Bible feels sharply out of step with our American culture and can appear pugnacious, even when stated with grace. This is about the doctrine of separation—biblical holiness in life and relationships.

I have watched with growing dismay as so many in the American evangelical church have cheerfully descended into theological illiteracy, lacking doctrinal discernment that is based on the careful study and application of the Scriptures. And the "problem is that even the mildest assertion of Christian truth today sounds like a thunderclap because the well-polished civility of our religious talk has kept us from hearing much of this kind of thing."[81]

In my conversations with younger Christian leaders, many of them raised in our own churches, they instinctively recoil at my mention of the doctrine of separation. Oh, they seem to understand that there are incorrect, even false, teachings . . . but they resist attributing incorrect or false teachings to actual teachers who are incorrect or false. That distinction seems too close to a personal attack. It is unkind, even intolerant. It is something that characterizes the previous generation. So our younger friends at first balk at the discussion, then they get silent, and ultimately they remain steadfastly unconvinced. They just aren't buying it.

I can somewhat sympathize. When I became a Christian in 1972, I felt similar emotions when I listened to older Christian leaders talk about the

---

81 David Wells, *No Place for the Truth* (Grand Rapids: Wm. B. Eerdmans, 1993), 10.

doctrine of separation. I thought many of those veterans of the Modernist-Fundamentalist battles seemed ungracious, angry, and mean-spirited. I agreed with their theology but disagreed with their attitude. I also thought that this doctrine received lop-sided attention from the men in our theological camp (the branch of American Christianity that I unashamedly embrace). Back then, many of my contemporaries thought the same, and as a consequence, the careful teaching of the doctrine of separation was largely ignored by my peers who believed it but didn't teach it. And this doctrine began its long descent into church-life-irrelevance.

Today, I'm concerned the doctrine of separation is being relegated to the dustbin of American church history. And in its place, the tolerant spirit of our day has become the most coveted of all character qualities, even by many in our churches. That may be culturally desirable, but is it biblical?

We need to restate the case for separatism to today's generation. I believe in recent years this doctrine has been neglected, ignored, or badly practiced with a spirit of carelessness on one extreme and an un-Christlike attitude on the other extreme.

The doctrine of separation must be presented as exegetically rigorous, logically coherent, faithful to biblical ecclesiology, and in a reasonable, non-parochial way that is practical and applicable. But is that possible? That's what this chapter attempts to demonstrate.

The Call to Purity

Clearly, God calls the follower of Jesus Christ to purity. We are called as individuals to holiness (1 Thess 4:7, 2 Tim 1:9). We are to be holy as he is holy (Lev 19:2, 1 Pet 1:16). We are to present our bodies to him in the pursuit of holiness (Rom 12:1). Our old man was crucified that we should no longer be slaves to sin (Rom 6:4–7). The new man is created in holiness (Eph 4:24). As 2 Corinthians states, "Let us cleanse ourselves from every defilement of body and spirit, bringing holiness to completion in the fear of God" (2 Cor 7:1).

The call to purity is the acknowledgment that God has called believers **out of** the world in order to maintain a personal and corporate purity **in the midst of** this world. Separation from sin is implied in the very word church: the Greek word *ekklesia* ("church") means "a called-out assembly."

The call to purity also is extended to the local church. In Christ's letter to the church of Pergamos, he warned against tolerating those who taught false doctrine (Rev 2:14–15). The elders of New Testament churches are commanded and warned by God to guard and protect the church from all manner of evil and wickedness. Acts 20:27–31 lays this responsibility before us:

> For I did not shrink from declaring to you the whole counsel of God. Pay careful attention to yourselves and to all the flock, in which the Holy Spirit has made you overseers, to care for the church of God, which he obtained with his own blood. I know that after my departure fierce wolves will come in among you, not sparing the flock; and from among your own selves will arise men speaking twisted things, to draw away the disciples after them. Therefore be alert, remembering that for three years I did not cease night or day to admonish every one with tears.of three years I did not cease to admonish each one with tears.

Personal separation relates to the individual Christian's call to purity. Ecclesiastical separation relates to churches and groups and the relationships between groups; it is not about individuals. Though ecclesiastical separation affects the lives of individuals, the term ecclesiastical by its very definition, is a term referring to churches, not individuals. The following general guidelines are presented for careful consideration regarding the position of the local church with reference to biblical separation.

Concerning Church Government and Organization

- Make sure that membership is granted only to those who are truly members of the body of Christ (Acts 2:41–47).
- Select for office and places of leadership only those who are spiritually mature and conform to the biblical standard of leadership (Acts 6:3–7, 1 Tim 3:1–13, Titus 1:5–9).

Concerning Disorderly and Sinning Brethren

- Seek to restore them in a spirit of love and meekness (Gal 6:1, 2).
- Lovingly discipline members who refuse to repent (1 Cor 5:1; 1 Tim 5:19, 20; Matt 18:15–17; 2 Thess 3:1–6).

Concerning Doctrine and the Gospel

- Guard the gospel as a sacred trust (1 Tim 1:1–11, 6:20; Gal 1:1–9).

- Refuse to allow unbelievers to have ministry of any kind in the local church (2 John 9–11, 1 John 4:1–6).
- Refuse to allow any who bring in false doctrine to have ministry in the local church (Rom 16:17, 18; Titus 3:9–11; 2 John 9, 10).
- Warn and speak out against false doctrine and false teachers (Phil 3:1–3, Acts 20:27–31, 1 Tim 4:1–16, 2 Tim 3:1–17).
- Preach and teach sound doctrine continually (2 Tim 3:16–17, 4:1–5).

Concerning Cooperation with Other Churches and Organizations

- Refuse to work in cooperation with churches or organizations that teach and promote doctrines which are contrary to the fundamental doctrines of the Word of God (Rom 16:17, 18; 2 John 9–11).
- Send forth only those missionaries who are known and adhere wholeheartedly to the doctrinal convictions of your local church (Acts 13:1–3).

Kevin Bauder has carefully examined that crucial passage in 2 John (a passage which is cited three times above).[82] Bauder's comments are instructive:

> [Second John verse 10] anticipates a situation in which a false teacher approaches a believer in order to propagate false doctrine. John's requirements are quite strict: believers must not receive this false teacher into their houses, nor must they bid the false teacher *chairein*. Whether the "house" is an actual dwelling or a house church is beside the point at the moment. The idea is that believers are not to open themselves to false teachers who come with the goal of propagating their doctrines....
>
> To encourage an enemy of Christ (even with so much as a civil greeting) is to gain a share in the evil that he does. In the context

---

82 Kevin T. Bauder, "Now, about Those Differences, Part 21: How Important Is Separation?" from his blog *In the Nick of Time* (first posted on Friday, 12 November 2010). Bauder's article cited here is but one in a long series of blog articles that he posted on the subject, and they carefully articulate the doctrine of ecclesiastical separation. Also, read Bauder's excellent contributions in *Four Views on the Spectrum of Evangelicalism* (edited by Andrew David Naselli and Collin Hansen, Zondervan, 2011). Bauder maintains that Fundamentalists are distinguished from other evangelicals primarily by their understanding of separation. I agree with him in that assessment.

of 2 John, such sharing in evil is precisely how a believer can lose reward.[83]

As Charles Spurgeon wrote regarding his struggle with doctrinal error and compromise in the nineteenth-century English Baptist Union in *The Sword and Trowel*, "Complicity with error will take from the best of men the power to enter any successful protest against it."[84] Elsewhere Spurgeon wrote, "It is our solemn conviction that where there can be no real spiritual communion, there should be no pretense of fellowship. Fellowship with known and vital error is participation in sin."[85]

I do not regard separation as a fundamental of the faith, and non-separatists are not necessarily denying the gospel. However, aligning oneself with the fierce opponents of Christ is never commendable.

In our days of doctrinal carelessness and toleration here in the twenty-first-century American church, the doctrine of biblical separation is mocked by many, ignored by most. But it is clearly taught throughout Scripture. Believers of all ages have received the same call to purity.

The Call to Balance

Clearly, the call to balance is given alongside the call to purity. The doctrine of biblical separation does *not* require Christians to avoid all contact with unbelievers. Like the Lord Jesus, we should befriend the sinner without partaking of the sin (Luke 7:34). Paul expressed a balanced view: "I wrote to you in my letter not to associate with sexually immoral people—not at all meaning the sexually immoral of this world, or the greedy and swindlers, or idolaters, since then you would need to go out of the world" (1 Cor 5:9–10). In other words, we are in the world, but not of it (John 17:11, 14–15).

The call to balance also means that we should exercise biblical separation with a humble, gracious spirit in such a way as to strengthen the body of Christ. After instructing Timothy to protect the church from false teaching (1 Tim 1:3), in the same context Paul wrote, "the aim of our charge is love that issues from a pure heart and a good conscience and a sincere faith" (1 Tim 1:5). Truth and love in balance. We see the same kind of balance in Paul's second letter to Timothy. After very strong words regarding the false

---

83 Bauder, "Now, about Those Differences."

84 Charles H. Spurgeon, "Notes," *The Sword and the Trowel* (October 1888).

85 Charles H. Spurgeon, "A Fragment upon the Down Grade," *The Sword and the Trowel* (November 1887).

teaching of Hymenaeus and Philetus (2 Tim 2:16–21), Paul instructed Timothy to pursue love and peace (2:22), to refuse to be quarrelsome (2:23–24), and to teach and correct with patient gentleness (2:24–25). That is balance.

Another sense of balance is needed when dealing with true brothers and sisters who genuinely know Jesus Christ as Savior but hold differing theological convictions. If you are a dispensationalist, can you enjoy a cup of coffee or pray with a charismatic or a covenant theologian? Can you live in the same town and maintain relationships on a personal level with Christians from other theological traditions? Balance dictates that the wise Christian can enjoy personal interactions with other Christians, even at times learn from them, and at times join with them in certain specific activities. But discernment dictates that our doctrinal convictions remain settled.

There is another element that needs to be balanced. Partnerships, networks, and collaborative efforts are vital (even God ordained) and must be established among believers and local churches. We must not use the negative aspect of the doctrine of separation to prevent the expression of the positive establishment of partnerships whenever possible. Whatever network of pastors and churches you choose to cultivate, it is vital you seek ministry partnerships where interdependence, not isolation, can be established. That is another balance to maintain.

Conclusion

Balance often seems absent from the church today, where extremes are all too common. Defensive, aggressive, mean-spirited provincialism is found on one extreme. And an undiscerning hyper-tolerance is found on the other extreme. We are called to purity **and** balance, a truth which seems largely forgotten by many in today's American church.

Believers can't escape the biblical mandate that we must discern the difference between the holy and the unholy relationship, the wise and unwise partnership. We are to be discerning and separated from sin while at the same time loving one another. We are to keep the call to purity in proper biblical balance.

Let us fellowship where we can. Let us separate where we must. Let us love one another no matter what.[86]

---

86 Adapted from Kevin T. Bauder, "Now, about Those Differences, Part 24: Fellowship and the Evangelical Spectrum," from his blog *In the Nick of Time* (first posted on Friday, 17 December 2010). He actually wrote it this way: "Let us separate where we must. Let us fellowship where we can. Let us love one another withal." I took the liberty to rearrange the order and change one word.

And this balance is never easily achieved. But it is a goal worth our every effort, for the Lord's glory and the sake of the gospel and the good of the church.

17

Responding to Cultural Decline

IN 1 TIMOTHY 4:16, Paul gives three commands to Timothy. The first command is that Timothy is to take heed to himself. The second command is that he is to take heed to his doctrine. The third command is that he is to continue in those two duties; in other words, he is to keep on taking heed to himself and keep on taking heed to his teaching, and never think that the days for personal vigilance are over.

Those sobering words echo in my mind as I observe current events swirling all about us and remember the historical context in which Paul wrote to Timothy. Our days are quite troubling, but so were the days for Paul and Timothy.

We have doctrinal decline in our American churches and moral degradation in our American society to such a degree that it can at times be overwhelming. How should America's pastors and churches respond? How are pastors going to train their congregations, and how will Christian parents train their children in a culture where profound evil and corruption and God-mocking perversion are pervasive, assumed, accepted, defended, de-stigmatized, and statistically normalized?

That's a great question, which was answered by Paul in 1 Timothy 4:16. Let me explain.

Historical Background

Nero was the Roman Emperor at the time Paul wrote to Timothy. Nero's rule was characterized by profound debauchery, misrule, and anti-Christian persecution.[87] He was a savage and heartless ruler who killed his mother,

---

87 Nero's vile wickedness is well documented and easily researched.

his fourteen-year-old step-brother, and one of his wives. He engaged in unspeakable, often public, perversions with men, women, boys, girls, and even with his family members. He married a number of times, including to a thirteen-year-old boy named Sporus whom Nero dressed up as a Roman empress while publicly parading him at his side. Nero threw murderous tantrums directed at family, friends, and rivals (real and imagined).

In one rather trifling incident compared to all of his other vile actions, Nero had a man's eyes gouged out simply for criticizing him. In a hugely significant incident, Nero ordered Rome to be burned so that he could rebuild it and rename it Neropolis. But that plan was exposed, and when he faced the backlash of Rome's citizens, Nero deflected blame and accused the Christians of starting the fire. As punishment, Nero ordered Christians to be thrown to dogs, while others were crucified and burned as human torches to light the night.

Tacitus was a Roman historian who was a little boy during Nero's rule. He has preserved a record of Nero's persecution following the fire in Rome, and we read this from his book *Annals*:

> And so, to get rid of this rumor, Nero set up [i.e., falsely accused] as the culprits and punished with the utmost refinement of cruelty a class hated for their abominations, who are commonly called Christians. Christus, from whom their name is derived, was executed at the hands of the procurator Pontius Pilate in the reign of Tiberius. Checked for a moment, this pernicious superstition again broke out, not only in Judea, the source of the evil, but even in Rome....
>
> Accordingly, arrest was first made of those who confessed [to being Christians]; then, on their evidence, an immense multitude was convicted, not so much on the charge of arson but because of [their] "hatred for the human race." Besides being put to death they were made to serve as objects of amusement; they were clothed in the hides of beasts and torn to death by dogs; others were crucified, others set on fire to serve to illuminate the night when daylight failed. Nero had thrown open his grounds for the display, and was putting on a show in the circus, where he mingled with the people in the dress of charioteer or drove about in his chariot. All this gave rise to a feeling of pity, even towards men whose guilt merited the most exemplary punishment; for it was

felt that they were being destroyed not for the public good but to gratify the cruelty of an individual.[88]

Certainly Nero was one of history's most vile rulers. But there's one last fact about Nero to consider. He ruled from AD 54–68, which meant he ruled when Paul wrote his letter to Timothy.[89]

In an empire ruled by the reprehensible Nero, Paul didn't bemoan the politics of Rome, nor did he command Timothy to march in protest. Instead, Paul commanded Timothy to pray for the emperor (1 Tim 2:1–2) and to select men with certain character qualities for church leadership who would, in turn, strengthen the church (1 Tim 3). And then in 1 Timothy 4:16, Paul commanded Timothy to attend to his personal life carefully and to pay careful attention to his teaching and to never think that the days for personal vigilance come to an end.

Two thousand years later, when the world is acting like the world, we may be tempted to despair. But 1 Timothy 4:16 reminds us that instead of reviling against the increasing wickedness that surrounds us, we need to be men whose spiritual lives are in order and who spend concentrated time at our desks doing the hard work of studying the Scripture. That's our duty before Christ.

Lessons from Paul's Response

I'm intrigued by how Paul acted during Nero's reign and how he commanded Timothy to act. But this was not unusual for Paul. He gave a similar command to Titus, to issue to the Cretans, whose history and culture were formed by pirates and mercenaries: "Remind them to be submissive to rulers and authorities, to be obedient, to be ready for every good work, to speak evil of no one, to avoid quarreling, to be gentle, and to show perfect courtesy toward all people" (Titus 3:1–2). The Cretans (who Paul called "liars, evil beasts and lazy gluttons" in Titus 1:12) were to be people who would take heed to their lives (Titus 3:1–2) and their doctrine (Titus 1:9).

---

88 *Complete Works of Tacitus*, trans. Alfred John Church, William Jackson Brodribb, and Sara Bryant (New York: Random House, reprinted 1942) Book XV, Chapter 44.

89 In fact, fifteen of the twenty-seven New Testament books were written when Nero was emperor. Only James, Galatians, 1 and 2 Thessalonians, Matthew and Mark were written before Nero's coronation. And Jude, 1–3 John, the Gospel of John and Revelation were written after Nero's death. All the other fifteen NT books were written with Nero on the throne in Rome; consider that background when reading those books of the NT.

Knowing the historical background, I'm also inspired by Paul's closing words in his letter to the Philippians: "All the saints greet you, but especially those who are of Caesar's household" (Phil 4:22). While Paul was imprisoned in Rome, he came to know the brethren, apparently more than a few, right there within Nero's Roman palace. Think of those brave brothers and sisters in Christ, seeking to live faithfully in that wicked house. That is an amazing thought and testimony of God's power to save even in the most desperate situations.

Yet, I also remember that even with all those exhortations, Nero had Paul beheaded. Despite a life of peaceful devotion to Christ and the gospel, wicked Nero acted the way the world acts toward holiness, righteousness, and truth.

Living in a world where profound evil, corruption, and God-defying perversion are pervasive—assumed, accepted, defended, de-stigmatized, and even considered statistically normal—is a constant challenge. But living in this kind of world has always been challenging for Christians, and 1 Timothy 4:16 underscores the extraordinary seriousness of the pastoral ministry. Paul's command to Timothy to attend to his personal life carefully and to pay careful attention to his teaching should move pastors to tenacious moral and theological vigilance while seeking to strengthen the church.

18

Blessings and Challenges of Rural Ministry

I'VE BEEN INVOLVED IN many different types of ministries over the past fifty years. In the United States, I've preached and taught in rural, small-town, suburban, and urban churches. I pastored a suburban church in Utah and a rural church outside of a small Indiana town. I've also served in a large church in an affluent suburb in North Carolina. Because of all this variety in my ministry, I've been interested in observing the differences in the ways that pastors and churches function in these different settings.

The culture and mindset of small-town/rural America are very different from the culture and mindset of urban/metro America. This poses some real challenges for pastors and spiritual leaders in rural churches. Here are a few of those challenges.

How to Disciple Men in the Rural Church

The problem with sin affects all men and women in all cultures. The Bible infers that the natural tendency of men is to be harsh, resentful, and bitter toward their wives and children (Col 3:19, 21). The Bible also infers that the natural tendency of women is to resist their husband's leadership (Col 3:18). The "battle of the sexes" is as old as the Garden of Eden (Gen 3:16). How does this age-old problem look in rural USA?

Rural men are often afraid of intimacy and transparency. They work alone. They're not skilled at communication. They allow the women to do all the talking and planning (since the men are out in the field anyway, and they are away from the telephone, and their wives are much more skilled at talking). So the wife arranges all the family details—calling the seed dealer and the Dairy Herd Improvement Association and the Co-op and the County Agent.

In a cultural mindset like that, the way Christian men relate to the church can be affected. The churches are all too often run by the women. Men see biblical spirituality as womanly/touchy-feely/emotional. Yet the Bible commands men to assume godly, loving leadership at home and in the church. The pastors must reach the rural men and disciple them into maturity.

The rural pastor needs to answer—where am I going to meet these resistant men and be with them, and how will I have a spiritual impact upon them?" Once they meet them and find ways to be with them, rural pastors must model biblical spirituality to rural men (1 Cor. 4:16, 11:1; Phil. 3:17, 4:9; 1 Thess 1:6; 2 Thess 3:7, 9).

At church, rural pastors need to teach and preach the Bible faithfully. God's Word is the sole means for spiritual growth for all men in all places at all times.

How to Plan Ahead in the Rural Church

The word "rural" is not about the size of a town (demographics or population numbers), nor the geographical situation (distance from urban/metro areas), nor the occupational description (a bunch of farmers and ranchers). Rather, you should define rural this way, with the following elements:

- the habitual way of thinking / perceiving / relating / evaluating,
- arising from a lifestyle and livelihood,
- which is directly dependent upon the land and / or the extraction of natural resources,
- which includes farmers, ranchers, shepherds, fishermen, loggers, miners,
- and to a lesser extent includes the people whose livelihood depends on serving the above.

Those with a rural mindset are entirely dependent upon resources not originating with people and are constantly reminded of their limited ability to control their destiny (due to conditions of weather, natural disasters, and market prices).

For the people with a rural mindset, in an environment where so many factors of success can't be controlled, the idea of planning seems presumptuous, even sinful. "Nobody can tell what is going to happen until it happens, so what's the point of setting goals?"

The goal for many in rural churches is maintenance not transformation, preservation not change. The small church world is essentially fixed and unchangeable, and progress means working out the bugs in the present way of doing things. What they value is living out the existing patterns of life and enjoying them to the full, not purposely planning by objective to achieve worthy goals for the future. Goal-setting is usually accomplished only by force upon rural folks from bankers and government agencies. These rural families have a natural prejudice against planning too far ahead.

When leading the church in planning ahead, the rural pastor should appeal to passages such as James 4:13–16 and Luke 14:28–32. Biblical authority will help our rural churches understand that planning is not always presumptuous sin.

Also, rural pastors should talk about guidelines rather than fixed and hardened goals. They should set biblically oriented, realistic, and attainable guidelines for the future and should resist coercion and manipulation in setting those guidelines. If those guidelines are not met, there should be no sense of failure or verbal punishment. There should always be plenty of room for adjustment, and if necessary, even abandonment, if outside factors beyond your control intervene.

How to Make Decisions in the Rural Church

The rural mindset is often "let's not discuss everything. I'll just do it, or you just do it." People with a rural mindset believe themselves to be CEOs who make their own decisions independent of everyone else. However, when group decisions must be made, they say, "let's all get along." In those times when group decisions must be made, the rural church's basic drive is, "let's not lose anyone from church as we make this decision." They want consensus. They want to talk around the edges of an issue. They want to discuss it but not debate it.

Rural pastors need patience during meetings. They need to master the art of gentle persuasion and asking questions (Prov 20:5). They need to avoid making motions by strictly following *Robert's Rules of Order* (which seems to them more like how to fight fair rather than how to discuss things). They need to avoid strong-arm tactics.

Rural pastors also need patience after the meetings. They should use meetings as a place for sharing information, then await the after-meeting discussions to take place (on the telephone or in the hallway or coffee shop) and seek to build consensus.

All the while behind the scenes, the rural pastor needs to be intentionally building male spiritual leaders who will assume godly leadership roles in the church to help him guide the decision-making process. He needs godly leaders to help him to build consensus.

Rural pastors who decide to implement change should:

- call attention to that which he perceives needs to be changed without proposing solutions (yet)
- allow dissatisfaction to build against the status quo
- build a consensus to make a change
- not appear to take sides (usually)
- avoid associating an issue with a person in the congregation (thereby making opponents within the church and forcing people to choose sides)
- not be in a hurry

How to Manage the Rural Church's Financial Resources

Few areas of rural church administration are as baffling to urban people as the management of money among rural folks. In the agrarian economy, profit margins are tight, production involves high risk with high investment, income is often at irregular intervals spaced as far apart as once a year, and spending is often done in lump sums. The ability to manage livelihood and meet family needs during prolonged periods without cash income is a matter of rural pride. Country folks carefully guard their cash reserves and use them only for emergencies or those things that are absolutely essential and urgent.

Rural pastors should approach the subject of money with extreme caution. Don't impale your pastoral ministry on the horn of the church budgeting process. Budgets often will be taken rather lightly, considered on the basis of available funds, and viewed as a reporting tool more than a ministry guiding tool. As trust builds between you and the people, you should explore ministry needs (not money needs) and let the conclusions of the people regarding those ministry needs suggest their intentional investment of money.

Spend money carefully and wisely. Your pastoral credibility will be measured by this yardstick more than perhaps any other in the country church.

As you are gaining trust, spend money on the things that contribute to survival, and later spend on the strategic biblical ministries.

Avoid debt. Rural folks are pressed by economic uncertainties, and they very likely will be troubled if the church consciously determines to go into debt for what they perceive to be "luxuries" (such as an overly ambitious building addition, purchasing new vehicles, extravagant parsonage remodeling). Urban people see mortgage debt as the normal way of advancing ahead; rural folks see mortgage debt as the first step to bankruptcy. And if debt *is* incurred, for the duration of the indebtedness, getting out of debt will be the main item on the ministry agenda (actually having the reverse effect instead of accelerating ministry).

How to Reach Newcomers Who Visit the Rural Church

Small churches tend to be family reunions. They are warm and caring if you are an established part of the group, but they also can be cliquish and unconcerned with newcomers outside the established group. Usually, the rural church is not intentionally opposed to newcomers, but you often would never know it by their actions.

Rural pastors need to show their people how to love strangers (literal meaning of 1 Tim 3:2, "hospitable"). They need to teach their church that newcomers aren't a threat to the status quo but an opportunity to minister God's Word and grace. They need to learn to reach beyond themselves unselfishly and intentionally with the love of God. Everyone needs to remember that the historic struggles and important events of your church congregation are not shared nor understood by newcomers.

Rural pastors should understand the differences in assimilating newcomers into rural churches as compared to urban churches. Newcomers break into small town churches by learning the story of the church's people and respecting their history. Newcomers break into city churches by learning the programs and respecting the mission statement.

How to Evaluate Ministries and Talent in the Rural Church

The standards of evaluation and perception of talent are different in rural churches than in urban churches. In the country, the exercise of talents is tied to survival or seen as a luxury that must await attention until survival needs are met. And since the rural economy demands such a high degree of labor and resource input, there is seldom an opportunity for polishing a talent to an extremely high degree.

On the other hand, urban churches, like most of America, demand excellence—and urban Christians buy into that philosophy without thinking through the effect upon less-than-perfect people. Rural life demands a general practitioner approach (resources, skills, and knowledge distributed over a wide and diverse range). Urban life demands specialization to achieve excellence. The level of development of talent and excellence of performance is radically different in the small-town church than in the urban church.

Rural folks know that some things "just must be done" (whether or not they're done perfectly). If a thing must be done, and if there's no one else to do it, they'll do it the best they can. ("If a thing is worth doing, it's worth doing, even if it's done poorly.")

Talent in rural churches is limited in quality and quantity. There are fewer numbers in the available talent pool. There is the lack of specialization among rural folks. The work week is highly demanding. The so-called "more talented people" often move away to the urban centers where they can develop their talent and receive the corresponding degree of reward.

Rural pastors need to remember that the church of Colosse was the smallest town among those receiving a New Testament letter, and it was commanded to do all things in the name of the Lord (Col 3:17) and they were to serve the Lord "heartily" or literally, "from the inner man, from the soul" (Col 3:23). Nothing was said to the small-town Colossians about excellence. We need to ask ourselves when the all-consuming drive for quality and excellence becomes an idol in America, even in our churches.

Rural pastors need to be cheerleaders. It's easy for people in the country church to think "I'm not good at anything," when they really mean, "I'm not highly specialized and truly excellent at any one thing." But rural pastors must not quit, believing there is no talent in the country church. Remember that God's investment in talent and gifts in the lives of his people far exceeds the normal utilization in all our churches—whether in city, town, or country.

Highly trained, gifted rural pastors and pastors' wives can easily discourage rural folks by unintentional intimidation. They think they're setting an example of excellence. But the rural folks in their congregation realize they can never match the pastor and his wife because the standard they've set is way beyond the normal rural folks' ability. This creates a dilemma: will the pastor and his wife become objects of admiration and awe, or will they become objects of jealousy and discouragement? The gifted rural pastor needs to reach out carefully to his rural folks with genuine Christ-like love and affirmation. Rural pastors need to give genuine encouragement to their multi-talented rural church folks.

What Should the Rural Pastor Seek in Character Qualities

The rural pastor should pursue *personal growth*: it's easy to go intellectually stagnant in isolated places.

The rural pastor should pursue *servanthood*: this is an essential character quality in out-of-the-way places.

The rural pastor should pursue *perseverance*: pastors don't tend to stay very long in small-town churches.

The rural pastor should pursue *contentment*: the glittering lights of bigger places can rob you of contentment in your small place.

Ministering the Word of God and modeling Christ-like leadership is always challenging no matter the setting, but it's also always rewarding. Certainly, many of the concepts above are cross-cultural and apply no matter where you may serve. Even big city pastors can learn from their rural pastor brothers. May Christ help all of us to be faithful as he builds his church—in the rural areas, small-towns, suburbs, and urban centers of our country.

19

Compassion and Poverty Ministry

IN 1972, I PLACED my faith in Jesus Christ as my Savior from my sin. Before my salvation, I was very much a product of the 1960s. Like so many others in my generation back then, many of us wanted to dedicate our lives to helping the poor, afflicted, and oppressed. I volunteered hundreds of hours to help the mentally disabled and those with Down syndrome. I worked to raise tens of thousands of dollars in my hometown to send to various agencies working with the poor here in the U.S. and in other countries. For two summers I served in volunteer social work in Appalachia and in Minnesota. I was preparing to get my university training with the determination to relieve poverty, hunger, and injustice.

Then something happened to me. I became a Christian. And my entire worldview changed—for which I will eternally praise God. But I've never forgotten my world in the 1960s, and in the years since my salvation, I've wondered how pastors should address the issues of poverty and local church ministry. What exactly does the Bible have to say about all of this?

What the Bible Says about the Poor

God established guidelines under the Mosaic law to help the poor. Exodus 22 and 23 told the Israelites to help the aliens, widows, orphans, and the poor. God wanted to protect their property, warned against showing favoritism which opposes the poor in favor of the wealthy, and set up a system of gleaning to help prevent starvation and malnourishment (Exod 23:10–12).

In Deuteronomy 15, we see God's intention was that his people would have all debts canceled every seven years. This was appropriately called "The Year for Canceling Debts." It also says, "there will never cease to be poor in the land. Therefore I command you, 'You shall open wide your hand to your brother, to the needy and to the poor, in your land.'" (Deut 15:11). God expected that his people would care for the poor.

God is called by many names throughout the Scriptures. It is interesting how many of his names emphasize his great love for the poor:

- Defender of the fatherless and widows (Deut 10:18; Ps 10:16–18, 40:17, 68:5; Jer 22:16)
- Protector of the poor (Ps 12:5)
- Rescuer of the poor (1 Sam 2:8; Ps 35:10, 72:4, 12–14; Isa 19:20, Jer 20:13)
- Provider for the poor (Ps 68:10, 146:7; Isa 41:17)
- Savior of the poor (Ps 34:6, 109:31)
- Refuge of the poor (Ps 14:6, Isa 25:4)
- For those who bless the poor, God promised to bless them (Ps 41:1–3, 112:5, 9; Prov 14:21, 31, 19:17, 22:9, 28:27; Isa 58:6–10).
- For those who oppress the poor, God promised to judge them (Deut 27:19; Prov 17:5, 21:13, 22:16, 28:27; Isa 10:1–4; Ezek 16:49, 18:12–13).

At the outset of his ministry, the Lord Jesus stood up in the synagogue at Nazareth and read from the prophet Isaiah: "The Spirit of the Lord is upon me, because he has anointed me to proclaim good news to the poor. He has sent me to proclaim liberty to the captives and recovering of sight to the blind, to set at liberty those who are oppressed, to proclaim the year of the Lord's favor" (Luke 4:18–19).

The four Gospels depict Christ repeatedly reaching out to those on the bottom of the social pyramid—poor people, women, Samaritans, lepers, children, prostitutes, and tax collectors. Jesus was also eager to accept people who were well-placed, but he made it clear that all, regardless of social position, needed to repent. For this reason, he invited the rich young man to repent of his idolatrous love of money, sell all of his possessions, and give the proceeds to the poor (Matt 19:16–26).

When he observed his disciples choosing the best places to sit at a wedding feast, the Lord Jesus used the occasion to address the issue of the poor and the social outcasts: "But when you give a feast, invite the poor, the crippled, the lame, the blind, and you will be blessed, because they cannot repay you. For you will be repaid at the resurrection of the just" (Luke 14:13–14).

Jesus himself cared for those in need by feeding the hungry. Crowds of four thousand (Mark 8:1–13) and five thousand (Mark 6:30–44) had assembled to listen to Jesus. They soon became hungry. When his disciples suggested that Jesus send the people away to buy food, he responded by saying, "I have compassion on the crowd," and "you give them something to eat." He then proceeded to perform miracles to feed these large crowds of hungry people.

The above represents just a small sampling. There are many other Bible passages with a great deal to say about how we should show works of compassion toward the poor and oppressed.

Of course there is a vital word of balance, and that is in regards to our ministry related to the Great Commission. We must keep in balance the priority to fulfill the Great Commission with the biblical command to show compassion. That priority of the Great Commission and Acts 1:8 should be given utmost emphasis in our ministries. But the question remains: how do compassion ministry and humanitarian work relate to the universal priority of proclaiming the gospel?

Compassion in the Bible

Compassion is an important concept in the Bible that can't be ignored.[90] In the Old Testament the Hebrew words *raḥum* and *ḥannun* are variously translated in our English Bibles as "mercy," "compassion," and "pity." Each of these words emphasizes a different aspect of compassion.

The root for the word *raḥum* is "womb, motherly feeling" and is used that way in Isaiah 49:15: "Can a woman forget her nursing child, that she should have no compassion [*raḥum*] on the son of her womb?" God uses the word *raḥum* in many passages to describe his compassionate mercy (Exod 33:19, 34:6; Neh 9:17a; Ps 86:15, 145:8; Joel 2:13; Jonah 4:2).

In Psalm 103:13 *raḥum* is used two times, once regarding human fathers with compassion and once regarding God the Father. The idea behind *raḥum* is that God is compassionate because of his character, as a loving father is compassionate toward his little child with feelings of love, kindness, and tenderness. But interestingly, this word is not used regarding how the rich are to respond to the poor.

---

90 I am deeply indebted to Dr. David J. Brown and his doctoral dissertation "Christian Ethics and Compassion Ministry to Orphans and Vulnerable Children in the Current AIDS Crisis in South Africa" (presented to North-West University, Potchefstroom University, 2011). His study shaped much of my own thinking in this section, and I want to give him full attribution.

The word *ḥannun* is the choice to be merciful by a superior toward an inferior, as used regarding God in Psalm 123:1–3a. As a defeated foe receives mercy from his conqueror when he is down, God the King of the universe sovereignly chooses to show mercy toward us. Interestingly, it is the word *ḥannun* that is used relative to how the rich are to regard the poor in Proverbs 14:21,31 and Daniel 4:27. If you have been blessed with finances, you are in a superior social position, but you should still choose to show mercy and demonstrate compassion toward those in a lesser social position.

So how does mercy relate to compassion? I found this distinction to be helpful: "Mercy refers to God's faithfulness. It is an act of the divine will. Compassion, on the other hand, refers to God's experience of suffering with the people's suffering."[91]

In the New Testament, the Greek word *splanchnizomai* is translated "compassion" and comes from the root word which means "inward parts, entrails, bowels."[92] John MacArthur notes this about the noun form *splanchna*:

> *splanchna* literally refers to the intestines or bowels. In Scriptures it is sometimes used literally, as when describing Judas' death (Acts 1:18). More often it is used figuratively to represent the emotions, much in the way we use the word *heart* today. The Hebrews, like many other ancient peoples, expressed attitudes and emotions in terms of physiological symptoms, not in abstractions. As most of us know from personal experience, many intense emotions—anxiety, fear, pity, remorse, and so on—can directly, and often immediately, affect the stomach and the digestive tract. Upset stomach, colitis, and ulcers are a few of the common ailments frequently related to emotional trauma. It is not strange, then, that ancient people associated strong emotions.

Obviosuly, *splanchna* is a very strong, even graphic, word!

Purves has written this about *splanchnizomai*: "Compassion in the New Testament literally means to have one's bowels turned over. The word refers to what we would perhaps call a 'gut-wrenching' experience . . . a feeling of solidarity with another that is virtually physical in its effect. There is nothing genteel or comely about compassion."[93]

---

[91] Andrew Purves, *The Search for Compassion: Spirituality and Ministry* (Louisville: Westminster/John Knox Press, 1989), 56.

[92] Bauer, Arndt and Gingrich, *A Greek-English Lexicon of the New Testament and Other Early Christian Literature*, 2nd ed. (Chicago: University of Chicago Press, 1979), 770.

[93] Purves, *The Search for Compassion: Spirituality and Ministry*, 18.

Compassion marked both the ministry and teaching of Christ. See his compassion on the multitudes (Matthew 9:36, 14:14, 15:32) and on the individually sick, demon possessed, and sorrowing (Matt 20:34; Mark 1:41, 9:22; Luke 7:13). Also note Jesus' use of the verb *splanchnizomai* regarding the compassionate work of the Good Samaritan (Luke 10:33), the compassion of the father toward the prodigal son (Luke 15:20), and the compassionate king in forgiving the debt of his slave (Matt 18:27). And he called those who would follow him to do compassionate works as he did (Col 3:12 tells us to "put on bowels of mercy" KJV).

The Actions of Compassion

The meaning of compassion is more than just feelings of sympathy, empathy, and pity. Compassion in the Bible is an emotion that compels action. Compassion is not sympathy nor empathy, although the words are quite similar in English. The main difference is in the level of personal involvement. Sympathy is a Bible word (*sumpatheō* in 1 Pet 3:8), but the word empathy is not used in the Bible (although the attitude is alluded to in Rom 12:15). Those two words keep things on the level of emotions, shared feelings. Sympathy and empathy mean we feel what the other person is feeling. However, compassion in the Bible is about active personal involvement that goes beyond mere emotions and shared feelings. Sympathy and empathy move a person to feel certain emotions; compassion moves a person to act.

Regarding this theologically significant verb, we have a big problem in our English language because English has no verbal forms for the word compassion. There is no English equivalent of the Hebrew and Greek words "to work compassion." In English you can't "compassion someone," so we miss the thrust of the Hebrew and Greek verbs. In English, you may be moved with compassion (noun) or may be described as compassionate (adjective). But in both cases it refers to an emotion within. To be accurate to the Bible, but inaccurate in English grammar, you would "compassionize someone." Nowhere does the Bible mention an example of someone having compassion and then doing nothing about it.[94]

So, biblical compassion must involve actions, and those actions are relayed to Christians in a superior social position who do acts of compassion toward those in a lesser social position. They "compassionize" them. They do works of compassion toward those in need.

---

94 Purves, *The Search for Compassion*, 15.

Of course, there is the vital need for balance in regards to our pastoral ministry related to the Great Commission. A recent trend in missions has been to gravitate away from the Great Commission passages (Matt 28:18–20, Mark 16:15, Luke 24:44–49, John 20:21, Acts 1:8) that Jesus purposefully gave as the theological foundation for carrying out his mission. Some have elevated other priorities in our mission efforts, such as social concern, humanitarian acts of kindness, disease abatement, or eco-justice.

May I never be guilty of advocating the de-commissioning of the Great Commission. But I do advocate for pastors to have a biblical balance. Pastors and churches must strive for balance in our ministries—fulfilling the Great Commission and obeying the biblical command to work compassion, striving for the biblical balance.

PERSPECTIVES ON NAVIGATING CHALLENGES

20

Success and Discouragement

ONE OF THE PASTOR's greatest struggles in ministry will be with himself and how he views his ministry. Doubts, fears, and discouragement paralyze even the best of pastors.

How the pastor defines success in ministry will help him deal with his inevitable struggles with discouragement. Therefore, it is essential that you understand what God says about success when evaluating your ministry.

Incorrect Assumptions about Success

It's an incorrect assumption that God will never give you a difficult assignment where "success" is elusive. Just one look at Isaiah's ministry (Isa 6:8–13), or Jeremiah's (Jer 1:8, 19, 7:26–27), or Ezekiel (Ezek 2:35, 3:711), or a whole host of others in the Bible will dispel that myth.

Another incorrect assumption is that God will always give us an assignment that enhances who we think we are, or who we think we should be. Sometimes we pursue success in ministry and assume it should be ours because we know God loves us and his love always leads to success. This misconception will lead to discouragement when the going gets tough in ministry.

A third incorrect assumption about success is that God somehow needs it from us. That is, we must be excellent and successful so God will look good. Such a view is a sinful magnification of ourselves and a trivialization of the Almighty King of Glory!

One final incorrect assumption about success is that it can be measured in numbers alone. As Americans we especially fall prey to this. But look at Noah—he preached one hundred twenty years (Gen 6:3), yet no one believed outside of his family. Was he a success? Was Jonah a success after the greatest revival in history (Jonah 3)? Did numerical success guarantee that Jonah would be happy in ministry (Jonah 4)?

Substitutions for Success

In our pursuit of success in ministry, we can seek the wrong things. In place of God's standards for success, we seek poor substitutions that will lead to discouragement.

Possessions

We sometimes substitute possessions for success, but the tangible things we possess in ministry can never measure our success. How frequently pastors look at church buildings, the size of the budget, the amount of salary, or the condition of our church vehicles (or other such things) as some measurement of our success in ministry. This can easily discourage.

Popularity

Another cheap substitution for success is popularity. How popular we are as a pastor in our church may or may not be an accurate measurement of our success in God's eyes. All of us love to be loved. Therefore, many pastors and churches incorrectly substitute popularity among people as a standard for success. Not all of God's choice servants are found in pulpits before thousands of listeners or have tens of thousands of followers on social media.

Power

A third substitution for success is power. Some pastors think that if they had a large staff working for them, or if they were one of the "movers and shakers" in ministry, then they'd be a success. But how can such a notion possibly exist when studying the example of Jesus Christ, the servant of all (Matt 20:25–28)?

Product

A fourth substitution for success is product—something to show for all your labors. The workman can measure his success at the end of a day by how much he produced. But what about the pastor? He works with people and their souls; how can this product ever be measured? Is it the pastor's fault when his people ("product") make sinful choices? Is my success as a pastor determined by how my people measure up as "my product"?

Standards for Success

God tells us about success in ministry, and determining his standards for success will clarify all of the above incorrect assumptions and cheap substitutions.

Obedience

Joshua 1:78 tells us that success in God's eyes first involves obedience to his Word. Note that Joshua was given his reminder from God when he was about to assume the leadership role that had been Moses' role. This becomes a stern rebuke to those in ministry who measure their success in comparison to others instead of in obedience to God's commands.

"Only be strong and very courageous, being careful to do according to all the law that Moses my servant commanded you. Do not turn from it to the right hand or to the left, that you may have good success wherever you go. This Book of the Law shall not depart from your mouth, but you shall meditate on it day and night, so that you may be careful to do according to all that is written in it. For then you will make your way prosperous, and then you will have good success." (Josh 1:7–8).

Faithfulness

The second standard for success is found in 1 Corinthians 4:2, where Paul writes that God requires His servants to be faithful. God's measure of success is not merely measured in achievement, but faithfulness to His call. Never forget this, pastor!

"Moreover, it is required of stewards that they be found faithful" (1 Cor 4:2).

Motives

A third standard God uses for success is in his measurement of our motives (1 Cor 4:3–5). Paul makes it clear—God will not only look at what we do, but also at why we do what we do. This is sobering when we pastors understand that God is one day going to expose the motivations behind our ministries. This is where Jonah failed after experiencing great numerical success. This is the very point at which some attempts at excellence fail—when our motivation is to be excellent for our own glory and our own reputation.

"With me it is a very small thing that I should be judged by you or by any human court. In fact, I do not even judge myself. For I am not aware of anything against myself, but I am not thereby acquitted. It is the Lord who judges me. Therefore do not pronounce judgment before the time, before the Lord comes, who will bring to light the things now hidden in darkness and will disclose the purposes of the heart. Then each one will receive his commendation from God" (1 Cor 4:3–5).

Perseverance

A fourth standard for success is perseverance (1 Cor 4:5). Paul warned all of us never to be premature in evaluating our ministry, because ultimate success would not be determined until the Bema Seat when we stand before the Lord himself and give an account to him. So, pastor, it is always too soon to quit obeying God, being faithful, and being Christ-honoring in your motives.

Lessons from Biblical Examples

Consider how the following servants of God were considered failures by the standards of the world, yet were faithful to their divine calling.

Jeremiah

Jeremiah's ministry spanned approximately forty years, yet he saw virtually no positive response. He was rejected, persecuted, imprisoned, and even dropped into a cistern (Jer 38:6). Most painful was witnessing the destruction of Jerusalem—the very judgment he had warned about for decades. From the world's perspective, Jeremiah was a failure; no one listened, and the disaster came anyway.

Yet from God's perspective, Jeremiah was entirely successful. He remained faithful to his calling despite overwhelming opposition. He continued to proclaim God's Word even when it brought him personal suffering. His obedience, not his results, defined his success.

Ezra

Ezra was another example of success, because "the hand of God was on him" (Ezra 7:6, 9). And why was God with Ezra? Because he devoted himself to studying, obeying, and teaching the Word (Ezra 7:10). What an example of success for pastors. What an antidote for discouragement—study, obey, and teach the Bible no matter what.

Paul

Consider the apostle Paul, who wrote from a prison cell, "I know how to be brought low, and I know how to abound. In any and every circumstance, I have learned the secret of facing plenty and hunger, abundance and need. I can do all things through him who strengthens me" (Phil 4:12–13).

Paul recognized that success wasn't defined by his circumstances but by his faithfulness to Christ. Despite imprisonment, beatings, shipwrecks, and ultimately execution, Paul could say at the end of his life, "I have fought the good fight, I have finished the race, I have kept the faith" (2 Tim 4:7). This is God's definition of success.

The Lord Jesus

Of course, the greatest "success" of all was our Lord Jesus Christ. Although hardly successful in the world's estimation, he nonetheless obeyed the Father, served others, and humbled himself into glorious exaltation (Phil 2:311). This is our example to follow as pastors, no matter the cost or discouragement.

Clearly men can be judged failures by others, yet glorious successes by God. This should encourage us in the midst of discouragement. The godly men above were all misjudged by their peers and considered unsuccessful at one time or another. The "others" of Hebrews 11:35–40 were colossal failures from the world's perspective yet glorious successes in God's assessment.

How can a pastor know when he's successful? In the final analysis, he can't in this life. This fact is clear from 1 Corinthians 4:25. Success or failure will not be determined in this life but will be determined at the Bema Seat.

Your eyes shouldn't be on your successes or your discouragements. Instead, you should faithfully persevere in studying, obeying, and teaching God's Word and leave all concerns about success in the hands of God. After all, he's the one we serve—not some group of people who are judging us, nor even ourselves. We should look for his words: "Well done, good and faithful servant," and those words will come only at the end of our ministries on earth.

21

Ethics in Ministry

THE ATTITUDES AND BEHAVIOR that resemble anything close to a biblical standard of ethics are crumbling in our society. Unfortunately, this moral decline is having a growing impact on pastors and the church.

With increasing frequency, I can identify the problems I hear about in churches as being related, in their root causes, to a violation of biblical ethics. And I can point to ethical violations on the part of church leaders, on the part of church congregations, and on the part of pastors. In some churches, tragic ethical violations have occurred at every level from congregation to leadership.

Why is this happening? Certainly, the root cause is the evil within each of us as human beings, which finds its expression in our own personal sin, selfishness, and carnality. As James wrote, "What causes quarrels and what causes fights among you? Is it not this, that your passions are at war within you? You desire and do not have, so you murder. You covet and cannot obtain, so you fight and quarrel" (Jas 4:1–2).

The most basic violations of ethics begin within the human heart. Sin poisons all activities of humanity. It is a fundamental principle within every person and the evil foundation of every relationship and activity within society. From our first parents in the Garden of Eden to the newborn infants who draw their first breath today, every human is infected with sin's rebellion against God and his Word.

Another root cause of ethical violations is the prevalence of the worldview that states there are no moral absolutes. Many people in our western world have adopted this philosophy, and it has severe implications for our society. Without the foundation of moral absolutes, there can be no ethical standards but rather personal preferences and agreed upon social contracts open to negotiation, subject to changing circumstances.

Some Relative Ethical Theories

When you state that you believe there are no absolutes, you are making an absolute statement, which in itself is logically absurd. You are also making the claim that there are only relative truths. And in a world of relative truth, as opposed to a world of absolute truth, how do you arrive at a standard of ethics? Here are a few of the answers given by the relative ethical theories we regularly encounter in American culture.

Majority Vote

In this case, morality and ethical behavior are determined by the majority of opinion. Statistics, opinion polls, and cultural relativism determine what is right. This is most often seen in the political arena, where fifty percent plus one vote is enough to determine the correct option when making decisions. But this ethical philosophy is also seen in many other expressions in our culture. It represents an ever-changing ethic based on the opinions of the day.

Intuition

This view states that right and wrong are emotive, implanted deep within each of us as human beings. Those who hold this view say there is no objective right or wrong based on some external standard. Rather, they say, within each of us is a common understanding and intuition of what is ethical behavior and "this is what makes us different from other animals, our innate, intuitive understanding of the morality and ethics of love and honesty and kindness."

Utilitarianism

This is the view that if something brings happiness and pleasure without pain, it is ethical and moral. They claim if something brings unhappiness and no pleasure but pain, it is ethically wrong and immoral. Actions are ethical, moral, and right in proportion as they tend to promote happiness. Actions are unethical, immoral, and wrong as they tend to produce the reverse of happiness. This view leads to materialism and hedonism (where pleasure or happiness is seen as the highest good).

Pragmatism

This view teaches that if it works, it's right. If it doesn't work, it's wrong. The ancient Chinese proverb best summarizes this view: "it doesn't matter if the cat is black or white so long as it catches the mouse." Those who hold to pragmatic ethics recognize no ultimate standard of morality beyond whatever proves useful for human purposes. They see that good values are those for which we have good reasons, based on whatever works. Pragmatism insists on usefulness or practical consequences as a test of truth and ethics.

Situation Ethics

This is a variation of pragmatism. This view teaches that morality and ethics are determined by the consequences of an act, and that each situation determines the correct and moral actions. Those who believe this teach that the act which brings the greatest good to the greatest number of people is most ethical and most moral. They believe that the moral worth of an action is determined by its outcome—the ends justify the means to that end, and this is based upon each situation. The result is a relative ethical standard that changes with each situation.

Behaviorism

This view teaches that man is the product of chance plus time (evolution), and he is a complex being of physical and chemical properties. Those who hold this view espouse that all behavior is physically and chemically determined and influenced by one's environment. Since physical/chemical factors, plus a person's upbringing/environment, control each human, there are no guilty people. No one can be blamed for his actions. As we often hear from those who hold this view, "there are no criminals, only criminal environments."

The Bible and Moral Absolutes

The most basic starting point for Christian ethics and morality is the fact that there is a God and he has truthfully revealed himself in an authoritative, written record called the Bible. And the Bible reveals that the eternal, holy God created everything in existence, including man. The Bible also reveals that man is morally and ethically responsible to this eternal, holy Creator God.

The revelation of God's moral law is given for his glory and the benefit of mankind. Inherent in all of God's moral laws is a consequence for disobedience, which is something he understands. So, obedience to God's ethics and morality will please the Creator, and it will also benefit the created.

Being responsible to God, man is given the expression of God's moral law and ethics in the Bible. Any infringement of God's moral laws as declared in the Bible is sin.

Ethical Principles

I am a dedicated ethical absolutist. I believe there are moral absolutes, and they are expressed in Scripture. Man is a responsible moral agent who will be judged on the basis of God's laws. He is not an animal helplessly programmed by his environment, genetics, and fate. He is a responsible person, not a mere cause-and-effect machine without moral accountability. This is the first and most basic step in understanding pastoral ethics and morality.

The second step is that we must be rigorous students of the Bible to learn God's moral laws and ethical principles. As we study and obey the Word of God, we are able to grow in the skill of thinking Christianly; we are able to grow in our ability to make appropriate ethical decisions, even in diverse and difficult situations.

Issues such as how we relate in our communities to those who do not believe and how we relate in church to our brothers and sisters in Christ become clear when we look to God's Word. The ethics of pastoral behavior, church leadership, and congregational life are clarified as we study what God says. The way we use our money, words, position, time, and talents all have ethical implications, and all are addressed in Scripture.

Below is a suggested statement of ethics for pastors and a similar statement of ethics for churches. These statements are broad and comprehensive, yet specific and rather detailed. They are an attempt to define what ethical commitment would look like in me as a pastor and in our like-minded churches. I hope that these statements will provide a tool for those who are concerned with holding the line, and perhaps even regaining it, in this important matter of maintaining a biblical standard in the war of ethics. May God help us to honor him in our churches and ministries, upholding his high and holy ethical standards.

A Sample Standard of Ethics for Pastors

The following standards are recommended in an effort to create a professional understanding and to preserve the dignity, maintain the discipline, and promote the integrity of our calling—the ministry of Jesus Christ as a pastor.

My Person

I will endeavor to pray regularly, to read, study, and meditate upon God's Word and maintain extended times of contemplation in pursuit of personal purity.

I will plan time to be with my family, realizing my special relationship to them and their position as important members of my congregation.

I will try to keep myself emotionally fit, keeping in control of my feelings and growing in my understanding of them.

I will strive to grow through comprehensive reading and participation in professional educational opportunities.

My Calling

I will seek to conduct myself consistently with my calling and commitment as a servant of God.

I will give full service to my congregation and will accept added outside responsibilities insofar as they do not interfere with the overall effectiveness of my ministry in the congregation.

I will treat all confidential matters as a sacred trust.

I will responsibly exercise the freedom of the pulpit, speaking the truth of God's Word with conviction in love; I will acknowledge any extensive use of material prepared by someone else.

My Finances

I will be honest in my stewardship of money, paying bills promptly, soliciting no personal favors or discounts on the basis of my position as pastor.

I will seek to have a cheerful spirit and refrain from complaining even in times of financial pressure, because I will trust the Lord to meet my needs in his time.

I will give offerings as a good steward and example to the church.

My Congregation

I will seek to regard all persons in the congregation with equal love and concern and undertake to minister impartially to their needs and refrain from behavior that will be divisive.

I will exercise confidence in the church's leadership, assisting in their training and mobilizing their creativity.

I will seek to lead the church in a positive direction to achieve the goals we have mutually agreed upon. I will remain open to constructive criticism and to suggestions intended to strengthen our common ministry.

I will humbly admit my mistakes of judgment and seek forgiveness when I have sinned against others in the congregation. I will also extend forgiveness to those in the congregation who have wronged me or my family.

I will seek to deal fairly and honestly with the church I am presently serving, even within the possible process of candidating for another ministry.

I will resign from the church if my doctrinal position changes from that of the church.

My Colleagues

I will not perform services in the area of responsibility of my colleagues in the Christian ministry except upon their request and/or consent.

I will, upon my departure, sever my pastoral relations with the congregation, recognizing that all pastoral functions should rightfully be conducted by my successor. I will seek to honor courtesy agreements made with fellow pastors.

I will, upon retirement or withdrawal from the ministry, refrain from engaging in pastoral functions within our church congregation unless requested by the pastor.

I will seek to maintain supportive and caring relationships with my colleagues in the ministry.

A Sample Standard of Ethics for Churches

The following standards are recommended in an effort to create an ethical understanding as we endeavor to preserve the dignity, maintain the discipline, and promote the integrity of our church. Endeavoring to uphold the constitution and bylaws of our church and recognizing Scripture as our final authority, we purpose that our manner of life will be worthy of the gospel of Christ (Phil 1:27).

Concerning Each Individual Member of the Congregation

> As a member of the congregation, I will endeavor to practice personal and family worship, training my children in the discipline and instruction of the Lord, and seeking the salvation of my family, friends, neighbors, co-workers, and acquaintances.
>
> I will endeavor, unless providentially hindered, to faithfully attend gatherings for worship, prayer, study, and fellowship, and will use my spiritual gifts for the common good.
>
> I will endeavor, by God's grace and power, to live as Christ in the world, denying ungodliness and worldly lusts. I will seek to fulfill my calling by leading a holy life being salt and light.
>
> I will endeavor to abide by the standards of sexual purity, ethical integrity, and spiritual fidelity as taught in the Bible.
>
> I will endeavor that in the event I am led away from membership in this church, I will maintain a spirit of grace as I diligently seek to unite with another church where I can serve as a member, and joyfully obey the principles of God's Word.

Concerning Our Congregation as a Whole

> We will endeavor through the power of the Holy Spirit to watch over one another in brotherly love, remembering one another in prayer, helping one another in sickness and distress, cultivating Christian compassion and courtesy, believing that the pursuit of peace with others and personal holiness accompany true faith in Christ.

We will endeavor to be slow to take offense, eager to seek the reconciliation Christ commands, and we will work to preserve the unity of the Spirit in the bond of peace.

We will endeavor to rejoice at each other's happiness and endeavor with tenderness and sympathy to bear each other's burdens and sorrows.

We will endeavor to participate faithfully in the ordinances of our church. We will both submit to the church's discipline upon ourselves and lovingly assume our responsibility to participate in the discipline of other members, as taught in Scripture.

We will endeavor to allow the Holy Spirit to put away our bitterness, wrath, anger, quarrelling, and slander; being kind to one another, in tenderheartedness forgiving one another, even as God, for Christ's sake, has forgiven us.

We will use the doctrinal statement and constitution of our church as our governing standards and the Scriptures as our final authority.

Concerning Our Pastor(s)

We will endeavor to love our pastor and his family, regularly praying for them.

We will endeavor to support our pastor's ministry by encouraging him and offering to share the burdens of his life and ministry.

We will endeavor to serve in the ministries of this church alongside our pastor, being eager to respond to his Scriptural leadership.

We will endeavor, when we disagree with our pastor, to do so with a spirit of grace and peace, discussing the issue privately with him, always respecting his biblical office.

Concerning Our Finances

We will endeavor to contribute cheerfully and regularly to this church for its general ministry expenses, the evangelism of the lost, the relief of the poor, the cause of spiritual growth and revival, and the spread of the gospel throughout all nations.

We will endeavor to generously and creatively provide for the financial and material welfare of our pastor(s) and any other staff we may call.

We will endeavor as a church to be ethical regarding business standards of financial accountability and above reproach in accordance with current legal practices and requirements.

We will endeavor to designate in our corporate dissolution clause ministries of like-minded faith and doctrine.

22

Creativity and Change in Ministry

CREATIVITY IN MINISTRY IS essential because times and circumstances change. Certainty in methods can paralyze implementing helpful and necessary innovations: "it is not the old who are wise, nor the aged who understand what is right" (Job 32:9). And there is one unalterable truth about life: "all flesh is grass, and its beauty is like the flower of the field" (Isa 40:6). As much as people may resist change, it most definitely and most regularly will come in this life.

Resistance to Change

What are some of the reasons creativity and change are resisted?

- It's an inborn universal human trait to resist change (*"I like things as they are"*).
- The unknown can be perceived as fearful (*"I don't know what it's going to be like"*).
- Nostalgic traditionalism fondly recalls the past (*"things were great back then; let's keep everything that way"*).
- Past successes can blind your vision for the future.
- The groups in control don't want to relinquish the status quo, which equals them retaining control.

Creativity in ministry can lead to excitement and success, but it will also lead to a lot of bad ideas that you'll scrap. Creativity can also lead to an emphasis on techniques and gimmicks, orienting your ministry toward indiscriminate changes and a de-emphasis on the Word and spiritual goals.

Not every change is good. In the Old Testament, the changes that King Rehoboam proposed after his father Solomon died led to a civil war. The change in kings from Ahaz (who was wicked) to Hezekiah (who was good) was a very beneficial change, but the change in kings from Josiah (who was the best king) to Jehoahaz (a terrible king who lasted three months) and to Jehoiakim (another terrible king who lasted eleven years) represented very bad changes.

Proverbs 22:28 is a good reminder about certain kinds of changes: "Do not move the ancient landmark that your fathers have set." In ancient Israel, boundary lines were sacred because all property was a gift from the Lord. The moving of boundary stones for the original writer of Proverbs 22 meant theft—theft from the owner of that land and disrespect for God, the giver of the land. By application, it's not too different for us today in many ways. Ancient boundary stones have always been meddled with, and many "boundary stones" today are being tampered with, moved, and even removed in ways that our forefathers would never have imagined.

It's tragic to observe we're now laughing at things that used to embarrass us thirty years ago. Mankind has always been tampering with boundary stones, moving them one way or another to suit his whims, sometimes removing them altogether. The cultural and intellectual elite purport to know best, and many of the undiscerning masses follow. "Get rid of that ancient boundary stone," all too many shout. "We don't need it anymore." Not all change is good.

Navigating Change Effectively

But, there comes a time for every ministry leader when they will want, even need, to initiate creative, new ideas. There are times when change is necessary.

Good ministry leaders don't wait for things to happen but creatively work to make things happen, as self-starters looking for ways to minister more effectively. Good leaders generate innovative ideas and inspire others to put them into action.

But this can be a tricky balance. On one extreme is the reality that failure can come from an excess of caution. While on the other extreme, it's just as true that failure can come from bold experiments with new ideas that are spectacularly unsuccessful. How do you maintain the balance?

Don't be afraid of new ideas and innovations, but don't get carried away with them too quickly. There's an old saying among pastors—churches are a lot like horses. They don't like to be startled or surprised. It causes defiant behavior. That's good advice for pastors in churches, as well as for ministry leaders of various kinds of ministries.

Strategies for Implementing Change

Here are ways to help reduce defiant responses from people when considering creative change:

Accept the fact that change is chaotic. The process of change is difficult to predict and often ends up being messy. Therefore, deal with change proactively rather than reactively, and be patient. Don't act surprised when things go haywire during the process of change.

Check your motives. Ask yourself "why do I want change?" This is as important as "what changes do I want?" Do you want to do something new so you'll become well-known and different from others? Or do you want to minister more biblically and more effectively?

Strategically choose the changes you make. Carefully determine the change you want to propose and then take the initiative. Begin to define the issues by starting with the sense of dissatisfaction with the way things are and pointing those things out. This becomes the window for change. Don't propose the change yet. You're just letting the folks on your ministry team see that something needs to change.

Go slow. When you are early in your ministry, don't make the mistake of proposing huge changes. They don't even know you yet, let alone trust you. Give them time to settle into your leadership before you begin proposing innovations and changes.

Start small. Begin with an easily attained change (i.e., "a winner"). Hopefully, this will go well and prepare the people for further creative innovations down the road.

Test the waters. When you think you're ready to consider a new idea or potential change, don't begin with a formal presentation of the change you want to make and how you will accomplish it. Just privately ask a couple key people and note their reaction. It tells what parts of the idea will receive the strongest resistance and who will be the strongest resisters.

Listen and respond to resisters. Listen to the resisters' push-back as an opportunity to turn a good idea into a great idea. These people will unintentionally shine and polish your idea by pointing out all the weaknesses way before any formal presentation. Don't start a debate, or even worse, a fight with the resisters. Listen to them and adjust your ideas as you wisely see fit.

Persuade the opinion makers. Secure strong supporters in advance—failing to do so is a serious misstep. Avoid putting people in the awkward position of voicing initial negative reactions in a public meeting, because once they go public with their less than positive opinion, it's hard for them to turn back and publicly accept your ideas about change. Publicly stated opinions are hard to walk back.

Decide before the decision. Continue to build quietly a consensus for the change and persuade others to own the decision before the decision/vote is made. Ideally, if a vote is required, the approval should be little more than a formality.

Guiding Principles for Change

The *controlling principle* for all the changes you propose must be the vision you have for your ministry. This vision will inspire people with a clear understanding of how things will be better with change. Think carefully about what you want to do and where you want to go, being absolutely certain that your vision is biblically based and God honoring.

Many spiritually minded, godly Christians find themselves uncomfortable with change because of the legitimate fear of encroaching pragmatism. The solution is to ensure that all change will fall within certain biblical parameters. And then you need to communicate this often. These five parameters include:

- holiness (Phil 3:10, 1 Pet 1:13–21)
- excellence (Phil 1:9–11)
- anticipation (Acts 1:4, 8, 14)
- relevance (1 Cor 9:19–23)
- teamwork (Phil 1:27, 4:2–3).

The *controlling attitude* for your ministry must be an attitude that shows you are eager to learn and improve. You need to demonstrate from the very start in your ministry that you haven't arrived, you don't have all the answers, you value input from anyone with good ideas on how to be more effective in ministry. Invite feedback. Solicit contrary opinions. Facilitate communication. This will show people how to adapt to change by modeling it yourself.

Learn to communicate the vision you have for your ministry in less than two minutes. Short and simple communicates better than long and complicated. Stating your vision to others in a concise way will allow you to get a reaction that signifies both understanding and interest. When you state it, your vision should motivate others to want to join your ministry team and get to work. And the ultimate result of people joining your ministry team will be that some things will change.

Great ministry leaders are those who do something. They're willing to risk failure because they truly believe something creative must be done. Navigating change is an important skill for a pastor to have.

23

Discernment in Ministry

SYNCRETISM HAS INVADED THE American church. Syncretism is the merging of different religious, cultural, and philosophical beliefs and practices into a new system. And syncretism was a tremendous problem in the Old Testament, where the people of God sinfully inter-mingled the religious beliefs and practices of the surrounding pagan nations into their worship of the true God. And this has been a problem every generation of God's people has had to battle ever since.

Syncretism Today

We live in a society that doesn't honor nor believe in absolute truth. Bible students are unsurprised to observe the spirit of this age in its rejection of absolutes.

But what is surprising is to observe how many professing believers have uncritically mixed error with truth (which is the definition of syncretism). For example, many professing Christians have syncretistically adopted the spirit of this age in the form of tolerance and non-judgmentalism. These people chafe against the idea of exclusiveness, in favor of inclusiveness. They urge us to be open and tolerant of all ideas. Some even think that all religious beliefs are equally valid and equally true and that it would be judgmental to assert one religious expression over another, even biblical Christianity. "We need to demonstrate more tolerance" is often the expressed attitude. Syncretistic thinking demands discernment on the part of true Christians.

Biblical Discernment

The word discernment is from the Latin word *discernere*, "to sift, to distinguish, to separate." It is the ability to distinguish between truth and error, right and wrong. Discernment is the separating process of making careful distinctions in our thinking about truth.

Every believer must develop the ability to discern the truth by rightly understanding the Scripture. We are to interpret the Scripture correctly. Then we are to apply it consistently to every circumstance we face in life.

Heresy and false teaching abound in our day, and we don't have to look far to see its impact. False teaching is rampant in the church, and Christians must correctly recognize it. Our judgments are to be made with adequate investigation and biblical discernment.

First Thessalonians 5:21–22 commands every Christian to be discerning: "But examine everything carefully; hold fast to that which is good; abstain from every form of evil." The apostle John issues a similar warning when he says, "Do not believe every spirit, but test the spirits to see whether they are from God; because many false prophets have gone out into the world" (1 John 4:1). Discernment is the ability to think biblically about all areas of life. Without it, Christians are at risk of being "tossed here and there by waves, and carried about by every wind of doctrine" (Eph 4:14).

As Christians, we are called to reflect thoughtfully, judge wisely, and be careful not to be seduced by the spirit of this age. Peter wrote that we are to "gird up the loins of your minds" (1 Pet 1:13), that is, we are to prepare our minds for action in the midst of a world hostile to the truth.

Renewing Our Minds

"Mind," "thinking," and "knowledge" are major subjects of New Testament revelation. Over forty different words are used to describe a person's intellectual life. Among these usages it is demonstrated that the unredeemed mind is "debased" (Rom 1:28), "darkened" (Eph 4:18), "deluded" (Col 2:4), "deceived" (Col 2:8), "corrupted" (2 Tim 3:8), and "defiled" (Titus 1:15). But the redeemed mind is "being renewed in knowledge after the image of its creator" (Col 3:10).

At salvation, the redeemed person is made a new creation (2 Cor 5:17) and as such is given a new mental ability to comprehend spiritual truth (Eph 4:20–24). Yet he still needs to readjust his thinking to align with the truth of the Bible, and he must always be on guard to avoid returning to sinful, unbiblical thinking.

Christians are to reject their old patterns and habits of thinking and replace them with a biblical mindset. This is exactly what Paul wrote in Rom 12:2: "Do not conform any longer to the pattern of this world, but be transformed by the renewing of your mind." This means that our thinking is not to be determined by the culture of the world around us, but instead we are to have a distinctly different and growing Christian evaluation of all we encounter in this life.

To think Christianly doesn't mean we think about Christian subjects only. Of course, it is from the foundation of revealed biblical truth and doctrine that we are able to think Christianly about other matters. However, having biblical discernment and understanding means that we think accurately, truthfully, and biblically, in a distinctively Christian way, about everything in this life. This is how a believer remains faithful when surrounded by a culture immersed in shallow thinking, mindless materialism, and self-gratification.

Doing Battle

We live in unthinking times when millions of people drift along through life, giving little thought to their souls, unaware of any way of thinking or living other than that of our secular culture. Yet this culture is called the *kosmos* in the Greek New Testament, which is the organized world system against God, energized and mobilized by God's enemy, Satan. There is an invisible war being fought on the level of ideas, philosophies, and cultural concepts, with Satan's goal being to oppose the truth of God in every way possible.

In 2 Corinthians 10:3–5 Paul described the war he fought "not according to the flesh" (v. 3). He wrote that he was "pulling down strongholds" (v. 4) and "bringing every thought into captivity" (v. 5) using two present participles to indicate this was a continuous activity, a never-ending battle. He wrote that his battle was against fortresses, prisons ("strongholds") which had been constructed on the level of "arguments" (v.5) or ideas, reasonings, philosophies. He "speared" (literally) every thought "into captivity to the obedience of Christ" (v. 5). Paul saw this as a most serious battle against human speculation, ideologies, lies, and false thinking. He knew that he had to think accurately, truthfully, and biblically, in a distinctively Christian way, about everything he encountered in life.

Like Paul, we need to engage in this warfare in a vigorous manner. Yet we must do so with love and grace and honesty. We must learn to say "I understand" before we say "I disagree." I fear that all too few of us care enough to work at understanding the messages we regularly encounter. And those of us who do understand are often afraid to disagree with the message out of fear of the messengers. But it is clear—we must do battle. And biblical discernment is the key.

An Appeal to Think Discerningly

In a day of frenetic exchange of information and a bombardment of messages, Christians need to slow down, think carefully, analyze every message through the grid of Scripture, and learn to be wisely discerning. We must continually make judgments and evaluations regarding everything we encounter to distinguish between what is true and wise as opposed to what is false and worthless.

We need to exercise discernment. In reality, Satan is behind many of these messages, in an attempt to conceal the glory of Jesus Christ and keep his prisoners behind the fortress of false ideology.

Discernment demands that we have a clear, uncompromising passion for the accurate teaching of God's Word. Because "Thy word is truth" (John 17:17), we must apply all skill and diligence in understanding what God has revealed, and so demonstrate a wise, godly reverence and fear. Syncretism has invaded the American church. Sloppy, careless thinking may overflow the shelves of our Christian book stores, but that is no excuse for the same to be happening in the pews of our churches!

Discernment is desperately needed in our world today. Are you willing to enter the never-ending battle for truth? Will you "love the Lord your God with all your heart, with all your soul, with all your mind, and with all your strength" (Mark 12:30)?

24

Attitude, Optimism, and Humor

Now in my seventh decade of life, I've come to deeply value the importance of choosing the right attitude. The words that follow, penned years ago, still resonate strongly with me.

> Attitude is more important than facts. It is more important than your past; more important than your education or your financial situation; more important than your circumstances, your successes, or your failures; more important than what other people think or say or do. It is more important than your appearance, your giftedness, or your skills. It will make or break a company. It will cause a church to soar or sink. It will make the difference between a happy home or a miserable home. You have a choice each day regarding the attitude you will embrace.
>
> Life is like a violin. You can focus on the broken strings that dangle, or you can play your life's melody on the one string that remains. You cannot change the years that have passed, nor can you change the daily tick of the clock. You cannot change the pace of your march toward your death. You cannot change the decisions or reactions of other people. And you certainly cannot change the inevitable. Those are strings that dangle! What you can do is play on the one string that remains—your attitude. I am convinced that life is 10 percent what happens to me and 90 percent how I react to it.[95]

---

95 Charles R. Swindoll, *Attitude: Your Most Important Choice* (Frisco: TX: Insight for Living, 1998).

This famous quote from Charles Swindoll highlights the power of your attitude in determining the outcomes of your life and ministry. While inspirational, we need to ask whether this perspective is biblically sound? An examination of Scripture reveals that a proper attitude of optimism is indeed central to faithful ministry and Christian living.

A biblical attitude is not merely positive thinking or emotional management; it reflects your theological understanding of God's sovereignty, goodness, and faithfulness. Our attitude derives from our understanding of God's character and his promises. Consider the following theological principles:

> **God's Sovereignty**: Romans 8:28 assures believers that "we know that for those those who love God, all things work together for good, for those who are called according to his purpose." When we truly believe God is in control, our attitude reflects trust rather than despair.
>
> **God's Goodness**: "The LORD is good, a stronghold in the day of trouble; and he knows those who take refuge in him" (Nah 1:7). A biblical attitude acknowledges God's essential goodness even when circumstances appear bleak.
>
> **God's Faithfulness**: Lamentations 3:22–23 reminds us that God's "mercies are new every morning; great is your faithfulness." Our attitude should reflect confidence in God's consistent character.

Scripture provides numerous examples of individuals whose attitudes either honored or dishonored God in difficult circumstances. Here are three examples in the Bible of a great attitude.

Ruth: Choosing Faithfulness over Bitterness

Following her father-in-law's death and her husband's death, Ruth had an exemplary attitude when compared to her mother-in-law Naomi's attitude.

Notice Ruth's response to Naomi: "Please don't press me to leave you or turn back. Wherever you go, I'll go; wherever you stay, I'll stay. Your people will be my people, and your God will be my God. Where you die, I'll die, and I'll be buried there. May the Lord punish me severely if anything but death separates us" (my paraphrase of Ruth 1:16–17).

In contrast, notice Naomi's response to the people of her hometown when Ruth and Naomi reached Bethlehem. The town was stirred, and the women asked, "Is this Naomi?" She replied, "Don't call me Naomi; call me

Mara, for the Almighty has made my life bitter. I went away full, but the Lord has brought me back empty" (my paraphrase of Ruth 1:19–21).

To fully appreciate Ruth's extraordinary attitude, we need to understand the gravity of her decision in its historical and cultural context. As a childless widow in the ancient Near East, Ruth faced severe economic hardship with few avenues for provision. By choosing to follow Naomi to Bethlehem, Ruth was leaving her native Moabite culture and entering Israelite society as an outsider. Her declaration, "your God shall be my God," represented a profound spiritual commitment to YHWH, abandoning the gods of Moab. Ruth had no guarantee of acceptance, remarriage, or provision in Bethlehem. And Moabites were specifically excluded from the assembly of the LORD "to the tenth generation" (Deut 23:3), making her decision even more remarkable.

Ruth refused to adopt her mother-in-law's bitter outlook, and ultimately, Boaz and all of Bethlehem took notice of her remarkable attitude and character: "And now, my daughter, do not fear. I will do for you all that you ask, for all my fellow townsmen know that you are a worthy woman" (Ruth 3:11).

Ruth's life powerfully illustrates the impact of the choices we make in shaping our mindset. Rather than dramatic interventions, God worked through Ruth's quiet, daily faithfulness—reminding us that seemingly ordinary attitudes can have profound and lasting significance.

Daniel: Excellence of Spirit in Exile

The second example of an excellent attitude is Daniel, whom Darius pulled out of retirement in 539 BC when Daniel was in his 80s: "It pleased Darius to set over the kingdom 120 satraps, to be throughout the whole kingdom; and over them three high officials, of whom Daniel was one, to whom these satraps should give account, so that the king might suffer no loss." (Dan 6:1–2).

The reason Daniel was so highly desired by Darius is given in the next verse: "Then this Daniel became distinguished above all the other high officials and satraps, because an excellent spirit was in him. And the king planned to set him over the whole kingdom. Then the high officials and the satraps sought to find a ground for complaint against Daniel with regard to the kingdom, but they could find no ground for complaint or any fault, because he was faithful, and no error or fault was found in him." (Dan 6:3–4).

Daniel was so highly regarded by the king because of these marks in his life:

- his excellent spirit (i.e., attitude)
- he was trustworthy (faithful)
- he was without error (he didn't do evil)
- he was without fault (he didn't neglect to do what he should)

Throughout his life, Daniel's excellent spirit was manifested in three other specific ways. He was consistent in his devotion—despite threats, "he got down on his knees three times a day and prayed and gave thanks before his God, as he had done previously" (Dan 6:10). He was respectful in submission—even to pagan authorities, Daniel maintained respect while remaining faithful to God (Dan 6:21–22). And he had a prophetic perspective—Daniel's attitude was shaped by his understanding of God's sovereignty in history (Dan 2:20–23, chapters 7–12).

Paul: Joy in Suffering

The third example of a great attitude is Paul, who demonstrated an extraordinary attitude throughout his ministry, particularly evident in his letter to the Philippians written from prison: "Whatever happens, conduct yourselves in a manner worthy of the gospel of Christ" (Phil 1:27). The phrase "whatever happens" is a reference to whether Paul can come to visit the Philippians or not. Paul gave this instruction so that "whether I come and see you or only hear about you in my absence, I will know that you stand firm in the one Spirit, striving together as one for the faith of the gospel" (Phil 1:27). No matter what unexpected disruptions, frustrations, or difficulties come our way, we are to respond with a Christlike attitude.

Later in Philippians Paul writes, "Your attitude should be the same as that of Christ Jesus" (Phil 2:5 NASB). When Paul instructs that our attitude should be the same as Christ's, Paul had summarized in the previous two verses what that attitude was: selflessness, humility, and service. "Do nothing from selfish ambition or conceit, but in humility count others more significant than yourselves. Let each of you look not only to his own interests, but also to the interests of others" (Phil 2:3–4). A hopeful, positive, unselfish attitude is so much more attractive in a pastor (and more honoring to God) than a negative, sullen, and selfish attitude.

Paul's attitude was characterized by his focus on Christ: "For to me to live is Christ, and to die is gain" (Phil 1:21). It was also characterized by joy despite circumstances: "Rejoice in the Lord always; again I will say, rejoice" (Phil 4:4). And his attitude was also characterized by contentment in all situations: "I have learned in whatever situation I am to be content" (Phil 4:11). These verses demonstrate Paul's exemplary attitude, which is a great example for pastors.

The Power of Optimism

In a world often marked by uncertainty and discouragement, the way we choose to see our circumstances matters deeply. For those in pastoral ministry, cultivating a hopeful perspective is not about denying reality or hardship, but rather it is about faithfully trusting in God and his ongoing work. This underscores the vital role of optimism.

Christian optimism differs fundamentally from secular "positive thinking." While the world roots optimism in human potential and improved circumstances, biblical optimism is grounded in God's character, his promises, his redemptive purposes, and the certainty of Christ's return and final victory. Biblical optimism connects directly to the theological virtues of faith (believing God's promises despite present appearances), hope (anticipating God's future actions based on his past faithfulness), and love (responding to God's goodness by extending it to others).

A positive attitude, which reflects an optimistic faith in God, is the practical expression of hope in our sovereign God. This hopeful spirit is absolutely essential to a spiritual leader. An optimistic pastor looks for opportunity, from God's hand, in adversity. Optimism is the ability to pursue goals persistently, despite setbacks; it is the practical application of faith in God's plan that leads to achievement.

Jacob's Pessimism: Example of Failed Leadership

Genesis provides a compelling case study in leadership failure through Jacob's pessimistic response to crisis. When his sons returned from Egypt, reporting that Simeon had been detained and Benjamin must accompany them on their return journey, Jacob exclaimed in despair, "All these things are against me!" (Gen 42:36). This moment of pessimism reveals several leadership failures.

First, Jacob's response demonstrates a profound theological blindness. Despite his personal history of divine encounters at Bethel (Gen 28:10–22), Peniel (Gen 32:22–32), and Shechem (Gen 33:18–20), Jacob failed to interpret his present circumstances through the lens of God's proven faithfulness.

His declaration that all things were against him directly contradicts the covenant promises God had repeatedly confirmed to him.

Second, Jacob's pessimism paralyzed decisive action. Rather than developing a strategic response to the crisis, his defeatist attitude led to a total shutdown and inaction that would ultimately affect his entire household. This fatalistic resignation demonstrates how pessimistic leadership affects, even endangers, others during critical moments.

Third, Jacob's response reveals self-centered leadership. His lament focuses on how circumstances affected him personally rather than considering his family's needs or Simeon's plight. The repeated use of first-person pronouns in his complaint ("me") reflects a leader whose perspective has narrowed to self-preservation.

The tragic irony, of course, is that these circumstances Jacob interpreted as against him were actually part of God's redemptive plan to preserve his entire family. Unknown to Jacob, his son Joseph was orchestrating events to reconcile the family and ensure their survival during famine. This narrative powerfully illustrates how pessimism blinds leaders to divine providence operating through apparent adversity.

Ministry leaders today face similar temptations toward pessimistic interpretation of challenging circumstances. Often we find ourselves bogged down by the harsh realities of current events that may not be in our favor. Under such circumstances, immature leaders retreat into dark discouragement and fail to acknowledge God's hand. They fail to look for the opportunities from God that their current hardships may present.

An optimistic pastor is aware that the current situation won't persist. Change will come, and given the right leadership attitude, it may even end up being for the better. Optimistic pastors see the big picture, viewing trials and tribulations as a small part of something bigger and favorable.

The Role of Humor in Pastoral Ministry

In moments of crisis, a pastor's thoughtful use of humor can be an effective shepherding tool bringing perspective, easing emotional strain, and creating space for people to breathe in the middle of frustration or crisis. When used wisely, humor can break the tension, help your congregation view a difficult situation through a more hopeful lens, and foster a sense of togetherness. It lightens burdens, lifts spirits, and enables people to stay focused and spiritually grounded when pressure threatens to overwhelm.

Though Scripture doesn't give direct commands about humor, it does affirm its place through key biblical principles. Our capacity for joy, laughter, and light-heartedness reflects the image of God in us (Gen 1:27), suggesting that even our sense of humor is part of his divine imprint. By definition, a sense of humor—the ability to perceive, enjoy, or express what is comical—is something we experience because God does. As pastors, we know that joy is a fruit of the Spirit (Gal 5:22), and appropriate humor can be one of its most natural expressions. Ecclesiastes 3:4 reminds us, "There is a time to weep and a time to laugh," affirming that even in ministry, even in crisis, there is a place for laughter and joy.

Humor serves multiple vital functions in ministry contexts. It provides crucial stress relief by offering perspective and emotional release during crises, allowing people to process tension in healthier ways. Well-crafted humor fosters connection and creates moments of authentic togetherness. Pastors can employ humor as an effective truth-telling vehicle, communicating difficult concepts or challenging feedback in more accessible and disarming ways than direct confrontation. When pastors use appropriate self-deprecating humor, they model genuine humility and create warmer relational bridges with their congregations. Perhaps most profoundly, humor often functions as an expression of theological hope, a defiant stance against darkness that affirms God's ultimate victory, allowing believers to laugh in the face of present trials because they confidently trust in their future hope.

The difficulty is that people perceive what is comical differently, and what sinful man often perceives as funny would not be funny to the holy and perfect God. Much of what the world calls humor is not funny but is crass and crude and should have no part in a Christian's life (Col 3:8). Other humor, such as sarcasm, is expressed at the expense of others (tearing down rather than building up), again something contrary to God's Word (Col 4:6, Eph 4:29). A good question to ask yourself—what elements of humor cross the line? Think carefully and biblically about the answer to this question, and then don't cross that line.

In summary, when used wisely by pastors, humor reflects the joy that remains our strength even in life's darkest moments. As pastors cultivate redemptive humor in our leadership, we offer our congregations not only momentary relief, but also a foretaste of the ultimate celebration awaiting God's people.

Conclusion

The three qualities of attitude, optimism, and humor function together in pastoral leadership. Attitude is the fundamental orientation of faith and obedience to God. Optimism is the specific expression of hope in God's promises despite circumstances, and humor is the grace-filled response that provides perspective and builds community. Together, they demonstrate a leader whose identity and security rest in Christ rather than circumstances.

Charles Swindoll's famous quote on attitude resonates because it reflects profound biblical truth. While circumstances remain beyond our control, our response to them—our attitude, our optimism, and our appropriate use of humor—remains firmly within our control and is a choice.

As Paul exhorted the Philippians, your attitude should be the same as that of Christ (Phil 2:5). This Christ-like attitude, characterized by humility, service, and joy, stands as both our goal and our witness. Through it, we not only experience effective ministry but also demonstrate the transformative power of the gospel we proclaim.

PERSPECTIVES ON THE LEGACY OF A SHEPHERD

25

Transitions and Successors

WHEN I WAS FIRST interviewed to become the next IFCA International Executive Director, the board asked me if I would be willing to serve for twenty years. "Twenty years?! Are you kidding me?" That seemed ludicrous and nigh unto impossible. After all, that date would be June 2019, and I was sitting at the table with those men in December, 1998. Such a thought was beyond my comprehension. But that's what they requested, and when I accepted the call to serve, I submitted to their request as from the Lord. So I put my head down and went to work, just like a farmer plowing a huge field that seems to stretch out of sight.

There was one thing that their request for twenty years of service did. It established a certain ending, a terminus for my service as Executive Director. The established date for my conclusion was built right into their call, and from the start began working towards finding God's man who would succeed me.

In all that has transpired over those twenty years, what did I learn about this process of leadership identification, development, and transition?

Moses and His Successor

I found quite helpful the things Hans Finzel wrote about the matter of leadership transitions and successors. He described the transition from Moses to Joshua, showing that leadership succession is nothing new.[96] In Numbers 27, near the end of his life, we read Moses asking God to find his replacement:

---

96 Much of the material in this section comes from Hans Finzel's article "All In or All Gone—Leaving Well When It's Time to Go." On Church Leaders website, https://churchleaders.com/pastors/pastor-articles/176730-hans-finzel-in-or-all-gone-leaving-well-when-it-s-time-to-go.html/2.

"Moses spoke to the LORD, saying, 'Let the LORD, the God of the spirits of all flesh, appoint a man over the congregation who shall go out before them and come in before them, who shall lead them out and bring them in, that the congregation of the LORD may not be as sheep that have no shepherd'" (Num 27:15–17).

Moses understood the reality we all have to face as leaders—there will be a day when we will no longer be the leader. Younger Joshuas and Calebs will succeed us, and we will step aside.[97] Leadership transition is a natural part of all ministry, and we need to proactively plan for it in order to make it as successful as possible.

But many ministry leaders are threatened by the notion of someone else taking over their position. It is instructive to note that when God called Moses at the burning bush to start his leadership assignment, Moses opposed the idea vehemently and gave God five excuses why he was not the man for the job. Fast forward forty years later—there was no argument at all when God told Moses he was done (Num 27:12–13). In fact, Moses prayed and asked God for the right successor. Reread Moses' prayer up above in verses 16–17. That's the kind of prayer every leader should utter to God: "Lord, help me identify those young emerging leaders coming up behind me to whom I can hand off the baton."[98]

God answered Moses' prayer and identified Joshua as the successor. Then God commanded Moses to publicly confer authority upon him: "So the LORD said to Moses, 'Take Joshua the son of Nun, a man in whom is the Spirit, and lay your hand on him. Make him stand before Eleazar the priest and all the congregation, and you shall commission him in their sight. You shall invest him with some of your authority, that all the congregation of the people of Israel may obey'" (Num 27:18–20). The transition from Moses to Joshua is such a helpful example, but what else does the Scripture teach about leadership and transitions?

All Leaders Are Replaceable

In a world of complicated demands that are limited by time and space, even the greatest of men and women can't get the job done alone. Collaboration is mandatory, especially at the leadership level. Collaborative leadership is where each member shares position and responsibility, and teams of gifted leaders serve together in pursuit of a clear and mutually compelling vision.

---

97 Finzel, "All In or All Gone."
98 Finzel, "All In or All Gone."

The opposite of collaborative leadership is solitary, single-handed leadership, which is monarchical rule or one-man leadership. Such a leader has little to no regard for his successor because his understanding of leadership is that everything revolves around him. In the political realm, he is called a tyrant, a dictator, or a king. This form of leadership is often adopted because it is simply easier to lead without the encumbrance of other people. Sadly, in other cases, some prefer to dominate others for their own power and personal glory. Others fight hard to maintain unchallenged authority because they have a deep-seated need to be needed. Still others feel they are the only ones who can get the job done right. And then some simply can't afford to step aside and lose the higher pay of a leader.

When you share leadership and look to find successors, you are making a statement—all leaders are replaceable. And those in ministry leadership have to admit that none of us are indispensable to the Lord's work. Therefore, we should work in collaboration with others and seek our successors because one day we will no longer be on the scene, and the work of God must go on without us.

Shared Leadership Is Biblical

The basic concept of shared leadership and searching for and training successors is biblical. The accomplishment of ministry in the New Testament was rarely done alone. Specifically, Paul wrote to Timothy that the ministry always involves training others who, in turn, will train others (2 Tim 2:2).

Local church leadership in the New Testament was to be done in plurality. Scriptural evidence indicates that the terms *elder*, *overseer*, and *pastor* all refer to the same person or leader (1 Pet 5:1–2; Titus 1:5,7; Eph 4:11). Elder refers more to the leader himself; whereas, overseer and pastor focus on the functions of the leader. Significantly, the word *elder* is primarily used in the plural form in the New Testament (Acts 14:5, Titus 1:5, Jas 5:14). This would indicate that the ruling body in each local church was a plurality of godly men identified as elders.

The concept of plurality of elders was present centuries before the New Testament. Leadership by a council of elders was a form of government found in nearly every society of the ancient Near East and it was the fundamental, governmental structure of the nation of Israel throughout its Old Testament history.[99] The Hebrew word *zaqen* is translated "elder" 135 times

---

99 Alex Strauch, *Biblical Eldership*, Revised and Expanded edition (Littleton, CO: Lewis & Roth, 1995), 39–43.

in the NASB, and it is used throughout the various eras of the Old Testament, beginning in Genesis 50:7 and Exodus 3:16, 18 and ending in Joel 2:16. For Israel, which was a tribal, patriarchal society, eldership was as basic as the family unit.

The apostle Paul was a Jewish missionary to the Gentiles, and he would've been thoroughly immersed in the Old Testament and Jewish culture. He followed the Hebrew pattern of plurality of elders for leadership in Acts 14:23 where he appointed elders (plural) in every church he planted (singular). These were councils of equals. A plurality of elders is the pattern we regularly find in the New Testament churches.

When you embrace the concept of collaborative and plurality leadership, you will always be seeking your successor and training him or at least laying the foundation for his success. And that's exactly what Paul told Timothy to do in 2 Timothy 2:2. Always search for new leaders to follow you, and then nurture them.

Barriers to Successors

Once the successor has been identified, the transition begins. But during the transition, there are barriers to success that the successor may encounter. Finzel has made the following observations in his book *The Top Ten Mistakes Leaders Make*:

> There are as many unsuccessful leadership transitions as there are successful ones. Everyone has witnessed firsthand a leadership transfer that went wrong. The reasons for such fiascos vary but most often include one or more of the following:
>
> - The organization doesn't like the new person.
> - The new person doesn't like the organization.
> - The new person's family can't adjust to the new city they moved to.
> - There is a corporate culture conflict: values and beliefs don't match.
> - The leader fails miserably in his newly assigned responsibilities: he lacks the ability, capacity, experience, or knowledge to do the job well.
> - The old guard sabotages the efforts of the new leader. Or the old leader sabotages the efforts of the new leader. Or the old leader fails to leave or reappears.

- The new leader lacks persistence in implementing changes. Or the new leader is recruited away by a better offer or challenge.
- The new leader fails to win a following because of poor interpersonal skills.[100]

That's a rather sobering list of barriers and pitfalls for any leadership succession. And all of us know from experience (either personal or observed) that Finzel has nailed it.

Conclusion

Leadership succession for a pastor is not an afterthought—it is an act of stewardship. God's work has always advanced through the faithful handoff of truth and responsibility from one generation to the next. From Moses to Joshua, Elijah to Elisha, Paul to Timothy, each transition reminds us that our role is temporary, but God's mission is eternal. Our task as pastors is to lead well while preparing those who will lead after us. That means praying earnestly for the right successors, training them diligently, and stepping aside gracefully when the time comes.

The measure of a leader's legacy is not how long he held the reins, but how faithfully he ensured the ministry would thrive in the hands of those who follow. May we lead with open hands, open hearts, and an unwavering trust that the Lord of the harvest will raise up His workers long after our race is run.

---

100 Hans Finzel, *The Top Ten Mistakes Leaders Make* (Wheaton: Victor Books, 1994), 157–178.

26

When They Leave Your Church

TENSION IN CHURCH, EVEN in the best of churches, is to be expected. The church where the Bible is faithfully taught at every worship service, where the people are serious about their love for Christ, and where their commitment to serve him is unwavering—yes, even those churches go through episodes of tension.

The reasons are many and varied, but like every family, the local church will experience stressful times. These times may involve differences of opinion (even arguments), financial pressures and hardships, building programs, changes in pastors or changes in programs or changes in the way things have been done, questionable decisions by leaders in various church ministries, differing preferences, sinful choices of people in the church, and many, many other circumstances. There is no doubt that tension in the church is to be expected.

Satan wants to divide the local church and bring shame upon the local testimony for Christ. Sometimes he stokes the fire of conflict when all that was present was tension. Remember, tension and problems in the church are not the same as conflict. The wise pastor knows the difference, and he seeks whenever possible "to maintain the unity of the Spirit in the bond of peace" (Eph 4:3).

But what is most difficult for every local church family is when people decide to leave the church. That is a unique tension that every congregation has to face. It's especially painful when those people are loved and appreciated yet still decide to go to another church. Their departure can be heartbreaking, leaving the congregation with questions and their (former) church family reeling. This is a tension few pastors like to address.

Reasons They Leave

According to God's plan, we're not called to serve alone, but rather we're called *together* as a local church to serve Christ *together*, as a body. Yet serving together can be challenging, stressful, and often exasperating.

Most of us would acknowledge that often the reasons people in America have for leaving a church are shallow and petty. Some people leave church because they don't like singing songs arranged in a musical style they don't like. Others leave because the color of the new paint or carpet was not their choice and they don't like the way the decision was made ("no one listened to me"). I know of people who left their church because the starting times for worship services and Sunday School were moved half an hour (in one church, the thirty minute change was earlier while in another church the thirty minute change was later).

Some left in anger over an issue long forgotten by all in the church but them. Some were forced out by heavy-handed and tyrannical leadership. Some leave out of boredom. I've heard all kinds of reasons for people leaving a church.

But are there legitimate reasons for leaving a church? As John MacArthur has written,

> There are times when it becomes necessary to leave a church for the sake of one's own conscience, or out of a duty to obey God rather than men. Such circumstances would include:
>
> - If heresy on some fundamental truth is being taught from the pulpit (Gal 1:7–9).
> - If the leaders of the church tolerate seriously errant doctrine from any who are given teaching authority in the fellowship (Rom 16:17).
> - If the church is characterized by a wanton disregard for Scripture, such as a refusal to discipline members who are sinning blatantly (1 Cor 5:1–7).
> - If unholy living is tolerated in the church (1 Cor 5:9–11).
> - If the church is seriously out of step with the biblical pattern for the church (2 Thess 3:6, 14).

- If the church is marked by gross hypocrisy, giving lip service to biblical Christianity but refusing to acknowledge its true power (2 Tim 3:5).[101]

According to those New Testament passages, there are legitimate reasons for leaving a church.

For Those Left Behind

Speaking from my own experience as a pastor, I can tell you how I felt whenever people left our church. My emotions ranged from sadness to embarrassment to confusion to a sense of betrayal to feelings of relief to a loss of confidence and a lot of second-guessing. As I quietly listened to the others in our congregation, I knew those emotions were shared by many others as well.

Why did we feel those emotions, and more? I think it's because of love. We loved those people, to a greater or lesser degree, depending on who they were and how long we shared our lives together. We counted them as important members of the body. We worshipped together, prayed for each other, worked together in ministry, and watched each other's families grow. We rejoiced when they rejoiced and cried when they cried—all because of love. And when our love was spurned (at least that's how it felt when they left our church), it hurt badly.

I suppose we wouldn't want it any other way, would we? What does it say about a church or a pastor when people can leave the church and no one cares, no one notices? Sadly, that does happen. Stony silence or cold indifference should never mark a Bible-preaching church. But how can pastors, leaders, and people respond when folks leave the church? What should we do?

One pastor, after some people left their church, quoted to the remaining congregation 1 John 2:19 ("They went out from us, but they were not of us; for if they had been of us, they would have continued with us. But they went out, that it might become plain that they all are not of us"). Another pastor eloquently recited Paul's sad report regarding Demas but applied it to those leaving their church ("Demas, in love with this present world, and has deserted me" 2 Tim 4:10).

Sometimes 1 John 2:19 and 2 Timothy 4:10 do apply to people who leave the church, but often that is not the case. They were of us. They didn't love this present world. They just left your church and are now attending an-

---

101 John MacArthur, "When Should People Leave Their Church?" https://www.gty.org/library/questions/QA120/When-Should-People-Leave- Their-Church.

other church. Do they deserve their former pastor saying, "as far as I'm concerned, it's good riddance to bad rubbish" (as one pastor said to his deacon board in my hearing, characterizing the people who left the church he pastored)? How should we pastors respond in these sad and awkward episodes?

A Lesson for Pastors

In my first full-time ministry after graduating from seminary, I was a missionary church planter in Utah. Ours was a congregation of less than twenty people when I first arrived, so I had a great deal of work to do in order to see the church become self-supporting. And I had a great deal to learn about being a pastor, so God allowed me to receive a ministry-altering lesson in my second month. It came during an intimate conversation with one of the great young couples of our church plant, Mark and Mary Ann.[102]

I went to Mark and Mary Ann's home for a get-acquainted evening. I was their new pastor, and like me, they were in their late 20s and were new parents. We had a number of shared interests, and we hit it off immediately. Their story of a rather recent conversion to Christ (about five years earlier) was especially compelling to me since that's why I was in Utah—to lead people to Christ, disciple them, and establish a vibrant local church. It caught my attention that they heard the gospel from another church in town. Ours was a suburb of a city with a metro area close to 175,000 people. But despite those numbers, as you can imagine in the state of Utah, there was a genuine scarcity of gospel-preaching, Bible-teaching churches. So their testimony caught my attention.

I asked some more questions about their involvement in that other church. They not only came to know Christ there, but they ultimately taught a Sunday school class, served in the youth ministry, sang in the choir, and took their turns as nursery workers. Ours was a church start-up, with hardly any ministries besides Sunday services. I quietly wondered, "why did they leave their former, established church where they came to Christ and served so faithfully to become a part of our small, little start-up church plant?"

Toward the end of the evening, I made a passing comment about how much that other church must have missed them when they left. I said something like, "good people like you are so hard to find, especially out here in Utah." Mark gulped a few times, and Mary Ann just hung her head in sorrow.

---

102 Mark and Mary Ann are not their real names. I have changed their names to protect their anonymity.

Mark responded, "They didn't say a thing when we left. We trusted Christ in that church. We were there every Sunday for five years in a row, and we did all those things. We thought they surely would have missed us. But they made some changes in ministry direction, and one Sunday we tried another church [the mother church of our church plant]. We liked it, and we've been gone now for almost two years. We still haven't heard anything from our former church." By that time Mark could hardly talk, and Mary Ann gently wiped tears from her eyes.

This conversation put me on the other side of church-leaving. I had been a pastoral intern and a youth pastor, so I was on the inside of discussions about what to do when people left the church. And those negative emotions like sadness, embarrassment, and confusion were the ones I imagined Mark and Mary Ann's former church must have felt. So I cautiously defended the lack of communication.

But Mark and Mary Ann insisted that somehow, someway their former church should have reached out to them. I asked, "But would it have made any difference in your leaving?" They said no, it wouldn't. Surprised, I asked, "Then why should they have contacted you?" And they said, "Because we wanted to know they loved us and missed us like we loved and missed them."

Then I told them how pastors always feel uncomfortable and awkward when people leave the church, and we're unsure what to do. They said that's just how they felt too. So I wondered, "Even with all that difficult emotion, you still think your former pastor should've communicated, even met with you?" Their response was a quick and simple, "Yes!"

A Course of Action

Those questions and their answers were burned into my mind, and I've never forgotten that lesson over all these years. I promised myself that night in Utah that whenever people left whatever church I was pastoring, I would do everything I could to communicate with them and extend a loving farewell to them. I haven't always been able to do that for various reasons, but it became one of those pastoral duties I tried my best to discharge faithfully.

Over the years, the manner of communication varied, and as I matured as a pastor, I think I got better at this difficult pastoral task. But I learned from Mark and Mary Ann that a pastor is still a pastor even as his sheep wander into another flock. And farewells are important among people who love each other. Words spoken (or not spoken) at farewells are long remembered, even written in granite.

After that night's lesson in Utah, here's the way I usually handled this delicate situation through the years. First, when I noticed or heard about some people's absence from church, I would usually ask around among the congregation about the status of the missing folks. Friends almost always know when friends are gone on vacation or are attending to family obligations. But if I heard a report that they were thinking of leaving the church, I paid special attention the next Sunday. If they were still missing, I'd call them on the telephone the next week. Immediately after the surprised (and sometimes cold) initial greeting, I would say (with as calm a voice as I could muster) that I missed them in church over the past couple weeks, and I heard they were thinking of going to another church and just checking to see if that was true. After some awkward silence, they would confirm the report. I would then ask if their decision was final, and if they told me it was, that's when my pastoral farewell began.

I would ask them the name of the other church they were considering attending. If it was a Bible-teaching church, I would tell them how sad I was that they were leaving our church and that I would miss them personally and our whole congregation would miss them. Then I would remind them of the areas of our church ministry where they served and how grateful we were for everything they had done in our church through the years. I would try to be as specific as possible in this recitation of their service—in the nursery or choir or youth ministry or on the missions committee or as a deacon or as a Sunday school teacher. Then I would tell them I loved them and encouraged them to continue to grow in grace and serve Christ faithfully no matter where they attended church. I would carefully avoid unkind words and an accusing, defensive attitude.

Then I would ask a very important question: "Have I done anything to offend or hurt you for which I should seek your forgiveness?" I didn't want them to harbor bitter feelings toward me if there was an unresolved issue between us. I didn't want The Chief Shepherd to find me guilty of mistreatment of his sheep. Thankfully, I don't recall ever having to ask for forgiveness from a family who'd left our church.

After we hung up (usually with a positive response on the other side), I would write them a personal letter expressing similar sentiments as I did on the phone. But I put those words into writing because I wanted my letter to become a rock of remembrance in their lives. They needed to know they were loved in our church, and we would miss them. But as their (now former) pastor, I was sending them off to continue in the lives I had urged them to live all the time that I was their pastor.

The practical benefit of such a send-off is that those left behind will hear about that farewell (and they will), and they will be content knowing their friends were given a loving farewell. This can dispel lingering doubts about the pastor's leadership. Often I would show the farewell letter to the elders and deacons so they could be assured how the ending was handled. Everyone seemed to appreciate my efforts, and I was satisfied that I was attempting to be a good shepherd of Christ's sheep, even as they departed.

Bad Partings

Of course, there are some cases in church when such a loving farewell is not possible. We had our share of church discipline cases, and we handled those differently, according to Matthew 18:15–18. When those people left, it was due to sin, and we prayed for their spiritual restoration. Other people left church simply to stop going to church and go fishing, or hunting every weekend, or sleep all day on Sunday, or to pursue other non-spiritual activities. Because such choices demonstrated a genuine spiritual deficiency in their lives, we continued to reach out to those people to bring them back to the flock. Many never returned.

Those left behind in church must be certain to handle the departure process in a godly fashion. I've heard about tremendous anger after some church partings, with all sorts of wreckage caused by the people who left and terrible words spoken to those who left by those who remained. The toxicity on both sides is devastating.

But it also works in other ways. The sheep aren't the only ones who leave church with a bad parting. One pastor felt wrongfully removed from the church, and as his final farewell, he outrageously trashed the parsonage. Other pastors who felt wronged by their congregations handled the post-breakup in a horrible, bitter fashion. No matter who does the leaving, and no matter the circumstances of the leaving, it never gives anyone the opportunity to dishonor the Lord and disobey his commands.

Concluding Thoughts

In an article entitled "Confessions of a (Recovering) Church hopper," John Fischer wrote these compelling words:

> In our free-market, commodity-rich society, it's understandable that we would approach church as we would a shopping mall of spiritual products and services. This is the way our culture operates.... As consumers we reserve the right to pass judgment on

the products and services we use, and the companies that service us begin to cater to our demands. "The customer is always right" may work well at McDonald's, but in a church it undermines the authority of the Word of God and the leaders God has called to represent Him. We do not go to a particular church to decide whether that church is doing everything right, but to hear from God and humbly find out where we went wrong that week in our own lives and what we need to do to make it right.[103]

Maybe some who leave your congregation are just church-hopping. That is an American Christian behavior, and it's not beneficial for anyone involved. But whenever people decide to leave your church, it is a unique tension. It is especially painful when those people are loved and appreciated yet still decide to leave. Their departure can be heartbreaking, leaving the congregation with questions and their (former) church family reeling.

This is a tension few pastors like to address. But it is nonetheless an important pastoral duty that must not be neglected.

---

103   John Fischer, "Confessions of a Recovering Church Hopper," *New Man* 3:1 (January/February 1996): 60–70.

27

Mission Drift

In my study of American church history, I've spent considerable time thinking how and why Christian churches and organizations gradually abandon their core theological convictions. There are all sorts of implications for us as pastors as well as implications for our churches, colleges, and ministry organizations. We need to consider the following words: "Without careful attention, faith-based organizations will inevitably drift from their founding mission. It's that simple. It will happen."[104] Those are severe words, but they can't be denied. They are substantiated by history.

Mission Drift in Colleges

There are countless examples of mission drift all throughout American church history. Perhaps the best-known examples involve America's original colleges.

Harvard is the oldest institution of higher education in the United States, established in 1636 by vote of the Great and General Court of the Massachusetts Bay Colony. It was named after the college's first benefactor, Presbyterian minister John Harvard, who upon his death in 1638 left his library and half his estate to the institution. A statue of John Harvard stands today in front of University Hall in Harvard Yard, and is perhaps the university's best-known landmark.[105]

In 1636, eight rules and precepts were observed at Harvard College. The second rule was "Let every student be plainly instructed and earnestly

---

104 Peter Greer and Chris Horst, *Mission Drift* (Minneapolis: Bethany House, 2014), 15.

105 Harvard University, "About Harvard: History," http://www.harvard.edu/about-harvard/harvard-glance/history.

pressed to consider well, the main end of his life and studies is, to know God and Jesus Christ which is eternal life, (John 17:3), and therefore to lay Christ in the bottom, as the only foundation of all sound knowledge and learning."[106] Thus, the first college in America was founded primarily as a religious school to train clergy in the Christian faith. Ten of its first twelve presidents were ministers.

The original motto of Harvard was "Truth (Veritas) for Christ (Christo) and the Church (Ecclesiae)." This motto was adopted in 1692, and the Latin words were part of their original seal. The motto and shield with this original language can still be found at multiple places on Harvard's campus.

Anglican minister James Blair established the second American college, the College of William and Mary. According to its charter of 1691, the college was started in order "that the Church of Virginia may be furnished with a seminary of ministers of the gospel, and that the youth may be piously educated in good letters and manners, and that the Christian religion may be propagated among the Western Indians to the glory of Almighty God."[107]

In 1699, ten Congregational ministers founded the Collegiate School of Connecticut (later renamed Yale) to further the faith. Yale University's charter in 1701 stated its purpose: "for the liberal and religious education of suitable youth . . . to propagate in this wilderness, the blessed reformed Protestant religion." Students were required to read Scriptures morning and evening at times of prayer.

In 1746, Princeton was founded by the Presbyterians with Rev. Jonathan Dickinson as its first president; famed theologian and evangelist Jonathan Edwards was the third president. Every Princeton student was required to attend worship in the college hall morning and evening.

In 1764, Brown University was established by the Baptists to further the revival now known as the Great Awakening in America. In 1766, the Dutch Reformed Church formed Queens College (now known as Rutgers University) teaching languages, liberal arts, and sciences especially to prepare students for the ministry. As you examine America's early history, churches and Christian leaders were *most often* the ones who founded our colleges and universities. And in the beginning, they were *almost always* the founders.

But things did not stay the same in America's first colleges and universities. In 1843 the motto of Harvard was changed to simply "Truth," and

---

106   Peter G. Mode, *Sourcebook and Biographical Guide For American Church History* (Menasha, WI: George Banta, 1991), 74–75.

107   *The History of the College of William and Mary, from Its Foundation, 1660 to 1874* (Richmond, VA: J.W. Randolph & English, 1874), 38.

the seal was officially changed. That symbolized the dramatic shift represented in all those original colleges. How did such wonderful institutions go from being training grounds for Christian ministers and respected citadels of higher education to what they are now? That's mission drift.

Mission Drift in Denominations

The late 19th and early 20th centuries saw the rise of higher biblical criticism and modernist theology, both of which questioned the authority and historicity of Scripture. A number of historic Protestant denominations embraced these perspectives, which led to doctrinal shifts, including a rejection of the inerrancy and authority of Scripture, the deity of Christ, the substitutionary atonement of Christ, the historicity of Christ's resurrection, and the reality of eternal retribution. These denominations fell under the influence of the Enlightenment, emphasizing reason and science against Christianity and encouraging skepticism toward traditional beliefs. The result was a denial of all supernatural aspects of Christianity to appeal to the educated elite.

At the same time, in the late nineteenth and early twentieth centuries, many American churches became involved in social reform movements, including the abolition of slavery, women's suffrage, and attention to the plight of the poor. While these movements reflected aspects of the ethical teachings of Christianity, the emphasis on social justice began to overshadow theological doctrines. This gave rise to the Social Gospel movement, which viewed sin more as societal injustice than individual guilt and rebellion against God, thus disregarding traditional teachings on sin and salvation.

In reaction to the above influences, the Fundamentalist movement emerged, upholding core and fundamental doctrines of biblical Christianity. But unfortunately, the protests of Fundamentalism did not halt the mainline Protestant denominations to continue their theological shift.

This drift in America's Protestant denominations wasn't called mission drift back then. Fundamentalists called it apostasy, which describes exactly the gradual abandonment of core theological convictions that mission drift describes. Mission drift ultimately ends in apostasy.

Mission Drift Describes Apostasy

The word apostasy is from the Greek word *apostasia*, which means "to rise up in open defiance of authority, with the presumed intention to overthrow it or to act in complete opposition to its demands—to rebel against, to revolt, to engage in insurrection, rebellion."[108] This word was used by Paul when he wrote "in the latter times some shall depart (verb form of *apostasia*) from the faith, giving heed to seducing spirits, and doctrines of demons" (1 Tim 4:1).

This overthrow or falling away from the faith is the very definition of apostasy. As in the first century, apostasy has always been a threat to the truth of God's Word in the body of Christ.

In Jude 3 we are urged "to contend for the faith that was once for all delivered to the saints." Jude then gives the reason for contending in verse 4: "For certain people have crept in unnoticed who long ago were designated for this condemnation, ungodly people, who pervert the grace of our God into sensuality and deny our only Master and Lord, Jesus Christ."

Apostasy comes with subtlety; note that Jude uses the word "crept." Peter says the false teachers "will secretly bring in destructive heresies" (2 Pet 2:1). Paul said such men are "false apostles, deceitful workmen, disguising themselves as apostles of Christ. And no wonder, for even Satan disguises himself as an angel of light" (2 Cor 11:13–14). In other words, don't look for apostates to have a wicked appearance on the outside or speak dramatically false words of heresy at the outset of their teaching. False teachers do not wear horns so we can identify them.

Some Reasons for Mission Drift

I can think of some reasons for mission drift, maybe not all of them, but here are four. The first reason is our adversary, the devil, is a liar (John 8:44) and seeks to deceive any and everyone possible by corrupting the truth. He actively snatches away the truth of God (Matt 13:19) and uses false teachers to confuse and mislead believers (Matt 7:15, Acts 20:29–30). In Matthew 13:24–29, Jesus said the devil sows professing believers among real believers like tares among wheat (tares are weeds which are similar in appearance to wheat). Sadly, until Christ returns and every spiritual enemy has been removed, tares such as these will be present among the wheat (Matt 13:30). These tares will try to halt God's work or at least push it into mission drift.

I believe a second reason for mission drift is our pride, believing this drift can't happen or won't happen to us in our lives or ministries. We mistakenly think, "We are above this happening because we are walking so closely with the Lord. It can't happen because we are so faithful." And in pride we

---

108 Johannes P. Louw and Eugene Albert Nida, *Greek-English Lexicon of the New Testament: Based on Semantic Domains* (New York: United Bible Societies, 1996), 495.

proceed ahead, maybe even rejecting the counsel and well-intentioned advice from brothers and sisters. We need to listen to the watchdog to see if it's barking at danger or just the moon. We better not shoot the watchdog because our pride tells us we always know better. Our pride can take us down a pathway we never intended for ourselves or our ministries.

Closely related to that second reason for mission drift is this third one: we become careless as we go through our ministry, and we make decisions with little or no forethought to how they will impact our future mission. We lose our careful discernment and fail to pay attention to the trajectory we're upon. We don't judge every one of our activities and decisions against the Word of God, and we end up on the slippery slope, incrementally drifting away.

A fourth reason for mission drift is when good people get caught up in the very real, daily pressures of life and ministry with its busy calendar, staffing and personnel issues, funding pressures, and a million other urgent matters. Instead of regularly stopping to reflect and consider where you're going and what's happening all around you, you go with the flow. And if things are getting desperate, sometimes in the fight to survive, ministry organizations make compromises to keep the doors open. You listen to large donors and accept their financial support (with the subtle strings attached, often including small or even great compromises). If you're not ever vigilant, over time, you will drift far from where you once were.

One Essential Caution

When considering reasons for mission drift, there's one essential caution to keep in mind—we can't confuse cultural issues with core doctrinal issues. Mission drift isn't about differences in cultural preferences or picking on godly friends over minor differences on insignificant issues. Preventing mission drift isn't about transforming mundane practicalities into precious issues of principle.

However, I am asserting that we must be careful to measure everything we do against the Bible. And if we can't find scriptural precedent for what we're doing and saying, and we have weak, unsubstantiated claims that can't stand up when challenged, then we'd better reassess what we're doing and saying. Perhaps we, in fact, do need to change. However, if there is scriptural support for the issues we are facing, then we need to stand strong no matter what others think.

Implications for Today

When I first studied apostasy in my early days as a Bible college student, it was mostly an academic exercise. My first pastor and then my Bible college professors were very explicit about the insidious nature of apostasy as they demonstrated historic and recent examples from the Bible and church history. I listened, and I learned. But much of it was beyond my mind to comprehend since I lacked practical experience in life and ministry.

It seemed inconceivable that I, or any ministry I would oversee, would ever forsake our central mission and purpose and untie ourselves from our strong scriptural moorings. But truthfully, I knew there is always in all of us, a gravitational pull downward and away from biblical orthodoxy to apostasy, from faithfulness to unfaithfulness. I knew that each church and ministry organization bears within it the seeds of its own destruction. And this gave me great pause.

But these words are very sobering indeed and they cannot be easily brushed aside when considering the historical reality they address.

It would be easy to write off Harvard and Yale's drift from their founding identity and purpose if they were exceptions, but mission drift is not relegated to the halls of Ivy League universities. Mission drift is a very real possibility for every organization. The zeal and beliefs of the founders are insufficient safeguards. There is no immunity, no matter how concrete your mission statement is. Or how passionate your leaders are. Or how much you believe it could never happen to you.[109]

I've reflected long and hard on these issues over my time in ministry. I've asked myself, "What do I need to be doing today that will help us to remain faithful stewards of the ministry entrusted to us? How can we prevent mission drift?" I know that one day I will give an account before the Lord at the judgment seat of Christ for my ministry leadership. These are crucial questions, and they remind all of us pastors and ministry leaders to take our stewardship from the Lord very seriously.

---

109 Greer and Horst, *Mission Drift*, 21.

28

Stewardship of Leadership

THE WORD STEWARDSHIP (*OIKONOMOS* / *"house"* + *"law"*) means to oversee and to manage someone else's property. In the ancient world, a steward was a slave who administered the master's household—supervised other slaves, handled business affairs, oversaw the finances, managed the household resources, and was the head manager, administrator.

For the Christian, Scripture proclaims that everything belongs to God: "The earth is the LORD'S, and all it contains, the world, and those who live in it" (Ps 24:1 NASB). Since everything we have is God's, we are mere managers for the Lord, even regarding our ministry. We need to have the attitude and the view that our ministry is his, just like our things are his things—all we have now, all we have lost in the past, and all we'll have in the future is his. It's as though God is merely leasing to us our property, money, relationships, talents, time, ministries, and even our lives. That means everything we are and all that we have are not ours to begin with. They belong to God. So, Christians must learn how to become responsible stewards of the resources entrusted into our care by God and manage everything to the best of our abilities for his glory. This fact has serious implications for the work we seek to do for God in Christian ministry.

Four Dynamics of Stewardship for Ministry Leaders

The first dynamic of stewardship is *the authority entrusted to the steward.* He is authorized by his master to exercise the work of the master and to employ the resources of the master according to the master's directive. All stewardship involves such authorization. In the parable of the talents (Matt 25:14–30), the master entrusted the servants with his property (talents) and authorized the servants to make good use of that property.

So also, with authority comes accountability. In Jesus's parable, we read "after a long time the master of those servants came and settled accounts with them" (Matt 25:19). He held the servants accountable for their use and investment of the talents. Paul emphasizes that accountability: "Moreover, it is required of stewards that they be found faithful" (1 Cor 4:2). The very identity of a steward requires one to be held accountable.

Thus, the first essential dynamic of stewardship—authority is received from the master and accountability is given to the master—becomes the foundation for the stewardship of Christian ministry. It represents the fundamental way Christian ministry leaders think about themselves and their ministry: your ministry doesn't belong to you, and one day you will give an account for the ministry entrusted to you.

The second dynamic of stewardship is *the responsibility to guard the owner's property*. Paul wrote to Timothy, his protégé in ministry, and exhorted him to "guard the good deposit entrusted to you" (2 Tim 1:14). The previous verse (2 Tim 1:13) makes clear that this deposit is the "pattern of sound words" which comprises orthodox doctrine based on the unadulterated Word of God. The point is this deposit has been entrusted to Timothy (as it was to Paul, see verse 12); that is, he is a steward of that deposit. No wonder the apostle later encouraged Timothy, "Do your best to present yourself to God as one approved, a worker who has no need to be ashamed, rightly handling the word of truth" (2 Tim 2:15). Note first that the object of Timothy's stewardship is the word of truth. This is where his authority lies, but there is also accountability, as Timothy's labor is to be approved by God. Colossians 1:25 says the same: "I became a minister according to the stewardship from God that was given to me for you, to make the word of God fully known."

The third dynamic of stewardship is *the care of people entrusted to the steward*. A pastor's primary stewardship is the care of those God has entrusted to him, attending to their spiritual growth and well-being. These are people with eternal souls, purchased by the blood of Christ; they belong to Him, not to the pastor.

In Acts 20, Paul summoned the elders of the Ephesian church to meet with him in Miletus. He exhorted them: "Pay careful attention to yourselves and to all the flock, in which the Holy Spirit has made you overseers, to care for the church of God, which he purchased with his own blood" (v. 28). Several insights are here.

First, the apostle encouraged the elders to watch themselves, indicating that they have a stewardship of their own lives and behavior before God. Ministry leaders are to steward their own personal lives first.

Second, these elders were to attend to the flock that is God's church. The flock doesn't belong to the elder but to God; it is God's flock and God's church, which he has purchased through the atoning work of Jesus Christ.

Third, God himself has placed the elders in this position of leadership and of stewardship, for the Holy Spirit was the one who made them overseers. Thus, they were authorized by God and accountable to him.

Similarly, Peter exhorted the elders of the Christian congregations in Asia Minor to "shepherd the flock of God that is among you" (1 Pet 5:2). As with Paul, Peter expressly identified the flock as belonging to God, not to human leaders. God is the owner of the flock; the elders serve as under-shepherds, as stewards.

The words of Hebrews 13:17 are not directed toward spiritual leaders but to the members of the congregations, exhorting them to obey and submit to their spiritual leaders. The reason given is that the leaders "are keeping watch over your souls, as those who will have to give an account." Accordingly, elders exercise a stewardship of the souls and the lives of the members of God's flock entrusted to them. Furthermore, these leaders are accountable for those souls and will give an account for them. This is a sobering reality for all who serve in Christian ministry.

The fourth dynamic of stewardship is *the faithful use of the steward's God-given gift*. First Peter 4:10 says, "As each has received a gift, use it to serve one another, as good stewards of God's varied grace." God has given different gifts to different people. No doubt this is what is meant in this passage when it speaks of God's varied grace. Accordingly, different people will demonstrate different giftedness. No one pastor excels in all the functions of ministry. In some areas, he will distinguish himself as exceptionally talented. In other areas of ministry, his work will be appreciated, but it is not out of the ordinary. The management (the stewardship) of ministry tasks must be attended to with an acute awareness of your strengths and weaknesses.

What Peter emphasizes in this passage (1 Pet 4:10) is that our gifts derive from God. Peter also emphasizes that these manifold gifts are to be used for God's purposes and glory "in order that in everything God may be glorified through Jesus Christ" (1 Pet 4:11). This infers stewardship. God is the source of the gift, and he provides the strength to use the gift. The gift is entrusted to a person in order to achieve the purpose of God in advancing his mission and edifying his church.

One other implication of 1 Peter 4:10–11 is that if you have been gifted by God, then you *must* faithfully use your gifts for his glory: "As each has received a gift, use it to serve one another, as good stewards of God's varied grace: whoever speaks, as one who speaks oracles of God; whoever serves, as one who serves by the strength that God supplies." If God has gifted you to be a Christian minister, then to do anything else is poor stewardship.

Principles of Stewardship from the Parable of the Talents

There are seven principles in the Parable of Talents that explain the nature of stewardship and inform the stewardship of leadership.

- Stewardship is a trust (Matt 25:14).
- A steward doesn't own the property (Matt 25:14).
- The owner does as he wishes with his property (Matt 25:15; Rom 14:4,8).
- Stewards face accountability (Matt 25:19, Rom 14:12).
- Faithfulness will be the standard of accountability (Matt 25:21, 23; 1 Cor 4: 2).
- Great faithfulness brings greater privileges, responsibilities (Matt 25:21b, 23b).
- Privilege unused is privilege removed; tragedy of wasted opportunity (Matt 25:24–29).

One Final Warning

In 1 Thessalonians 2:4, Paul writes, "just as we have been approved (*dokimazō*) by God to be entrusted with the gospel, so we speak, not to please man, but to please God who tests (*dokimazō*) our hearts." God tests us and entrusts us with ministry (v. 4a). Then he continues to test us (v.4b).

But in 1 Corinthians 9:26–27, Paul writes, "I do not run aimlessly; I do not box as one beating the air. But I discipline my body and keep it under control, lest after preaching to others I myself should be disqualified (*adokimos*)." If you abuse your stewardship as a Christian minister and disqualify yourself, God will remove your stewardship from you. That is a sobering truth.

29

Resilience, Perseverance, and Endurance

YOU MUST NEVER FORGET ministry is war, and you'll never serve successfully in Christian ministry if you live with a peacetime mentality. The fundamental battle of pastoral ministry isn't the battle with the shifting values of the surrounding culture. It's not the struggle with resistant people who don't care for the gospel. It's not the fight for the success of the ministries of the church. And it's not the constant struggle of resources and personnel to accomplish the mission. No, the war of the spiritual leader is a deeply personal war that Satan desires you to lose. It's fought on the ground of the leader's heart. It's a war of values, allegiances, and motivations.

This war is the greatest threat to every pastor and Christian worker, yet it's a war that we often naively ignore or quickly forget in the busyness of ministry. In the war that ministry leaders face, we must develop a wartime mentality and soldier on despite hardship, opposition, and struggles.

When Great Men Despaired

Even the strongest leaders in Scripture experienced moments of deep despair. The godly men below were in such despair that they actually wanted God to take their lives.

Job (Job 3:20–23; 6:8–9). Job faced terrible circumstances: the death of all his children, the loss of his wealth, and the deterioration of his health. His overwhelming grief drove him to question why God allowed him to continue living in such pain.

Moses (Num 11:10–15). The burden of leading the constantly complaining Israelites became too much for Moses. He felt overwhelming responsibility that drove him to despair, pleading with God to take his life rather than continue bearing such a heavy load.

Elijah (1 Kgs 19:4). After his amazing triumph over 850 false prophets at Mount Carmel, Elijah experienced physical exhaustion and hunger. His overwhelming victory ironically led to a deep post-triumph depression, particularly when facing Jezebel's threats.

Jonah (Jonah 4:3, 8). When God showed mercy to Nineveh, Israel's enemy, Jonah was filled with anger and resentment. The overwhelming mercy of God toward those who Jonah believed deserved judgment caused him to prefer death over witnessing such forgiveness.

Jeremiah (Jer 20:14–18). Jeremiah faced relentless persecution for boldly proclaiming God's message, enduring such intense opposition tha he was driven to curse the very day of his birth and wish for death. His ministry, marked by intense sorrow and suffering, is often overlooked when we consider examples of perseverance and endurance in Scripture. Yet Jeremiah stands as a profound model of faithful endurance—a prophet whose life and message deserve deeper reflection and study.

Jeremiah's Trials and Perseverance

Jeremiah faced incredible trials throughout his prophetic ministry. During King Josiah's reign, reforms were implemented, and many people returned to God. However, many others inwardly resented these changes. When King Josiah died, his reformation was quickly undone, and people openly defied God while plotting against Jeremiah because of his faithful proclamation of God's Word.

Jeremiah experienced rejection from every quarter:

- By his neighbors (11:19–21)
- By his family (12:1–9)
- By his fellow priests (20:1–6)
- By friends (20:7–10)
- By his audience (26:7–8)
- By kings (36:20–26)
- Jeremiah endured numerous hardships:
- Death threats (11:18–23)
- Isolation (15:17b)
- Commanded to remain unmarried and childless (16:2)

- Beaten (20:2a)
- Placed in stocks (20:2–3)
- Taunted (28:10–11)
- His written work was burned (36:23)
- Imprisoned six times

Jeremiah's Imprisonments

All of Jeremiah's six imprisonments occurred in 586 BC as the Babylonian army besieged Jerusalem, leading to its capture and destruction. After Jerusalem fell, Jewish exiles fled to Egypt, forcing Jeremiah to go with them:

- Arrested at the gate and committed to a dungeon on false treason charges (32:2; 33:1; 37:11–15)
- Released from the dungeon but restricted to the prison courtyard (37:16–21)
- Imprisoned in Malchiah's miry dungeon/cistern in the prison courtyard, left to starve (38:1–6, 9)
- Released from the cistern but restricted to the prison courtyard until Jerusalem fell (38:17–28)
- Taken in chains to Ramah by the Babylonian guard, then released (40:1–4)
- Taken by force to Egypt after Jerusalem's destruction (43:4–7)

How Jeremiah Found Strength to Persevere

Jeremiah's experience offers powerful insight into what it means to cultivate resilience in ministry. The book of Lamentations, written by Jeremiah in the aftermath of Jerusalem's catastrophic destruction in 586 BC, exposes the depth of Jeremiah's grief while also revealing the foundation of his unwavering hope. In the ruins of everything he cherished, Jeremiah discovered that true endurance is anchored not in circumstances, but in the unchanging character of God.

Jeremiah's Anguish (Lam 3:1–20)

In verses 1–17, Jeremiah expressed his deep anguish of heart over the judgment of God in the destruction of Jerusalem. In his anguishing description of his profound grief, we see that by verse eighteen, all hope seemed to be gone for Jeremiah.

Jeremiah's Anchors (Lam 3:21–24)

But in his anguish, Jeremiah found hope when he "recalled to mind" (v. 21) these four truths about God:

- ḥesed ("LORD's lovingkindnesses," v. 22a): God's covenant loyalty regarding his promises brought Jeremiah great comfort.
- raḥûm ("compassions," v. 22b): God's motherly feeling of compassion toward his people is demonstrated in this word, which comes from the same root word as "womb."
- 'emûnah ("faithfulness," v. 23b): God is steady, reliable, dependable all of the time, and this attribute of God means he can be depended upon.
- ḥeleq ("LORD is my portion," v. 24a): God is enough, even in devastating circumstances; this word also refers to an allotment of land that provides all the necessities of life.

When Jeremiah intentionally focused his heart and mind on these four unchanging truths about God, his inner turmoil and anguish were replaced by a steadfast confidence and hope (vv. 21, 24). His example shows us that in moments when life's circumstances tempt us toward despair, we must make a conscious decision to shift our focus from emotion to truth. We anchor our hope not in changing feelings, but in the unshakable character of God—his steadfast love, tender compassion, unwavering faithfulness, and the sufficiency of himself. These four anchors that Jeremiah had also provide us today with the perspective to persevere.

Principles for Perseverance in Ministry

Persevering in ministry requires us to cling to principles rooted in Scripture and shaped by a God-centered perspective. Ministry is filled with challenges that can discourage and debilitate even the most faithful servant. The following seven biblical principles offer practical wisdom and spiritual strength to help leaders endure in ministry with faithfulness and resilience.

1. Maintain a Theocentric Perspective.

Like Jeremiah in Lamentations 3:21–24 and Paul in 2 Corinthians 4:1–16, we must maintain a God-centered view of our circumstances. When our focus shifts from ourselves to God's character and promises, we find the strength to endure. Keeping our focus on the eternal rewards and glory promised by God helps us to endure present sufferings (2 Cor 4:17–18).

2. Reject the Philosophy of Solo Leadership.

Leadership becomes a lonely task for the solo leader. This is why Scripture consistently presents a pattern of shared leadership in the church. The wisdom of Ecclesiastes 4:9–12 highlights the benefits of team leadership. A leadership team can carry the responsibilities more efficiently and effectively, preventing burnout. Jethro's advice to Moses remains applicable today: "You and these people who come to you will only wear yourselves out. The work is too heavy for you; you cannot handle it alone" (Exod 18:18).

The mindset of the solo leader leads to the sense of being irreplaceable, which subtly erodes both our effectiveness and our longevity in ministry. It breeds exhaustion, fosters unhealthy pressure, and ultimately paves the way for burnout and resignation. When we carry what God never intended us to bear alone, we risk collapsing under the weight of self-imposed expectations.

3. Have Faith in God's Promises.

Endurance is strengthened by unwavering faith in God's promises and faithfulness (Rom 4:20–21). When we believe that God will fulfill what he has promised, we find courage to continue despite difficulties. Faith shifts our focus from what we see to what God has said. Trusting in his Word allows us to persevere with confidence, even when the outcome is not yet visible.

4. Develop Patience in God's Timing.

Patience is crucial for endurance, requiring us to wait on God's timing rather than demanding our timing (Col 1:11). The biblical concept of patience involves active endurance, not passive resignation. It's true that God often works in seasons, and his delays are not denials—they are opportunities to grow deeper in trust. True patience acknowledges that God's timing is perfect, even when it stretches us beyond our comfort.

5. Understand There Is Joy in Trials.

Embracing joy amidst trials helps us to endure, knowing that our suffering produces perseverance and character (Jas 1:2–4). This counterintuitive response to hardship transforms our experience of suffering. Believing there is joy in trials doesn't deny pain; it declares purpose in the midst of it. By choosing joy, we affirm our confidence that God is working even through our adversity.

6. Seek Strength through the Holy Spirit.

The Holy Spirit empowers us to endure beyond our natural abilities (Eph 3:16). We can tap into supernatural resources that sustain us when our human strength fails. The Holy Spirit renews our inner being day by day, giving us spiritual resilience for the long haul. Through the Spirit, we gain divine perspective and power to keep going when we feel like giving up.

7. Acknowledge Your Ultimate Role Model Is Jesus Christ.

Jesus, knowing the suffering he would endure, nevertheless persevered through his ministry, culminating in his crucifixion and resurrection for our salvation. In the Garden of Gethsemane, he prayed, "Father, if you are willing, take this cup from me; yet not my will, but yours be done" (Luke 22:42). Hebrews 12:2 instructs us to fix our eyes on Jesus, "who for the joy set before him endured the cross, scorning its shame, and sat down at the right hand of the throne of God."

Jesus' perseverance through suffering for a greater purpose and his obedience to the Father teach us to endure hardships for the sake of fulfilling God's will and plan.

Conclusion

Ministry is not a sprint—it's a long and often challenging journey marked by trials, fatigue, and spiritual warfare. The pressures can be intense, and the temptation to quit can feel overwhelming. But God hasn't called us to endure in our strength. He has provided timeless principles, grounded in his Word and revealed through the lives of faithful servants, to equip us for resilience.

As we fix our eyes on the Lord's character, lean into the strength of the Holy Spirit, embrace the support of godly leadership, and follow the example of Christ himself, we are empowered to press on with endurance. The battle may be fierce, but our calling is clear—and our God is faithful. Until Christ returns or calls us home, may we run the race with joy, serve with perseverance, and remain steadfast in the ministry entrusted to us.

AUTHOR'S BIOGRAPHY

Dr. Les Lofquist grew up in Winona, Minnesota and was educated at Grand Rapids (MI) School of Bible and Music (Diploma, 1976), Grace College (Bachelor of Arts, 1979), Grace Theological Seminary (Master of Divinity, 1982), and The Southern Baptist Theological Seminary (Doctor of Ministry, 2023).

He served as a church planter at Roy Bible Church in Roy, Utah, a Bible college professor in Grand Rapids, Michigan, and as a part-time seminary professor at Grace Theological Seminary of Winona Lake, Indiana where he also served as Senior Pastor at Pleasant View Bible Church.

Then for twenty years he directed the fellowship of IFCA International with over 1500 churches, pastors, Christian workers, chaplains, mission agencies, and eight Bible colleges and seminaries in twenty-seven countries. During those years, he was also editor of *VOICE* magazine.

In June 2019, Les and his wife Miriam moved to Cary, North Carolina where he joined the faculty of Shepherds Theological Seminary and the pastoral team at The Shepherd's Church, where he serves as Executive Pastor.

Les and Miriam have five adult children, four of whom are married, and seven grandsons.

Made in the USA
Middletown, DE
24 September 2025

17499042R00116